THE COMMONITORY OF VINCENT OF LERINS

For the Antiquity and Universality of the Catholic Faith Against the Profane Novelties of all Heresies:

Translated by
Rev. C. A. Heurtley, D.D.,

Edited by
Paul A. Böer, Sr.

VERITATIS SPLENDOR PUBLICATIONS
et cognoscetis veritatem et veritas liberabit vos (Jn 8:32)

MMXII

This is a re-publication of a work found in:

A Select Library of the Nicene and Post-Nicene Fathers of the Christian Church, Second Series, ed. Philip Schaff, LL.D. (Buffalo: The Christian Literature Co., 1886). Vol. 11 Sulpitius Severus, Vincent of Lerins, John Cassian   The contents of which is in the public domain.

However, this excerpted version is copyrighted.

AD MAJOREM DEI GLORIAM

TABLE OF CONTENTS

Introduction. 9

Chapter I. The Object of the Following Treatise.
.... 20

Chapter II. A General Rule for distinguishing the Truth of the Catholic Faith from the Falsehood of Heretical Pravity. 25

Chapter III. What is to be done if one or more dissent from the rest. 27

Chapter IV. The evil resulting from the bringing in of Novel Doctrine shown in the instances of the Donatists and Arians. 29

Chapter V. The Example set us by the Martyrs, whom no force could hinder from defending the Faith of their Predecessors. 35

Chapter VI. The example of Pope Stephen in resisting the Iteration of Baptism. 39

Chapter VII. How Heretics, craftily cite obscure passages in ancient writers in support of their own novelties. 44

Chapter VIII. Exposition of St. Paul's Words, Gal. i. 8. 48

Chapter IX. His warning to the Galatians a warning to all. 50

Chapter X. Why Eminent Men are permitted by God to become Authors of Novelties in the Church.53

Chapter XI. Examples from Church History, confirming the words of Moses,--Nestorius, Photinus, Apollinaris..56

Chapter XII. A fuller account of the Errors of Photinus, Apollinaris and Nestorius.................61

Chapter XIII. The Catholic Doctrine of the Trinity and the Incarnation explained............................64

Chapter XIV. Jesus Christ Man in Truth, not in Semblance. 69

Chapter XV. The Union of the Divine with the Human Nature took place in the very Conception of the Virgin. The appellation "The Mother of God." 72

Chapter XVI. Recapitulation of what was said of the Catholic Faith and of divers Heresies, Chapters xi-xv. 76

Chapter XVII. The Error of Origen a great Trial to the Church. 79

Chapter XVIII. Tertullian a great Trial to the Church. 86

Chapter XIX. What we ought to learn from these Examples. 90

Chapter XX. The Notes of a true Catholic..... 91

Chapter XXI. Exposition of St. Paul's Words.--1 Tim. vi. 20. 94

Chapter XXII. A more particular Exposition of 1 Tim. vi. 20. 97

Chapter XXIII. On Development in Religious Knowledge. 99

Chapter XXIV. Continuation of the Exposition of 1 Tim. vi. 20. 104

Chapter XXV. Heretics appeal to Scripture that they may more easily succeed in deceiving. 109

Chapter XXVI. Heretics, in quoting Scripture, follow the example of the Devil. 113

Chapter XXVII. What Rule is to be observed in the Interpretation of Scripture. 116

Chapter XXVIII. In what Way, on collating the consentient opinions of the Ancient Masters, the Novelties of Heretics may be detected and condemned. 118

Chapter XXIX. Recapitulation. 124

Chapter XXX. The Council of Ephesus. 127

Chapter XXXI. The Constancy of the Ephesine Fathers in driving away Novelty and maintaining Antiquity. 130

Chapter XXXII. The zeal of Celestine and Sixtus, bishops of Rome, in opposing Novelty. 133

Chapter XXXIII. The Children of the Catholic Church ought to adhere to the Faith of their Fathers and die for it. 135

Introduction.

Very little is known of the author of the following Treatise. He writes under the assumed name of Peregrinus, but Gennadius of Marseilles, [398] who flourished a.d. 495, some sixty years after its date, ascribes it to Vincentius, an inmate of the famous monastery of Lerins, in the island of that name, [399] and his ascription has been universally accepted.

Vincentius was of Gallic nationality. In earlier life he had been engaged in secular pursuits, whether civil or military is not clear, though the term he uses, "secularis militia," might possibly imply the latter. He refers to the Council of Ephesus, held in the summer and early autumn of 431, as having been held some three years previously to the time at which he was writing "ante triennium ferme." [400] This gives the date of the Commonitory 434. Cyril, bishop of Alexandria, was still living. [401] Sixtus the Third had succeeded to the See of Rome; [402] his predecessor, Celestine, having died in 432. Gennadius says that Vincentius died, "Theodosio et Valentiniano regnantibus." [403] Theodosius died, leaving Valentinian still reigning, in July, 450. Vincentius' death, therefore, must have occurred in or before that year.

Baronius places his name in the Roman Martyrology,
Tillemont doubts whether with sufficient reason. [404]
He is commemorated on the 24th of May.

Vincentius has been charged with Semipelagianism.
Whether he actually held the doctrine which was
afterwards called by that name is not clear. Certainly the
express enunciation of it is nowhere to be found in the
Commonitory. But it is extremely probable that at least
his sympathies were with those who held it. For not only
does he omit the name of St. Augustine, who was
especially obnoxious to them, when making honorable
mention at any time of the champions of the faith, but
he denounces his doctrine, though under a
misrepresentation of it, as one of the forms of that novel
error which he reprobates. [405] Indeed, whoever will
compare what he says in S: 70 of the heresy which he
describes but forbears to name, with Prosper's account
of the charges brought against Augustine by certain
Semipelagian clergymen of Marseilles, [406] will have
little doubt that Vincentius and they had the same
teacher in view, and were of the same mind with regard
to his teaching. Be this however as it may, when it is
considered that the monks of Lerins, in common with
the general body of the churchmen of Southern Gaul,
were strenuous upholders of Semipelagianism, it will not
be thought surprising that Vincentius should have been
suspected of at least a leaning in that direction.
Tillemont, who forbears to express himself decidedly,
but evidently inclines to that view, says "L'opinion qui le

condamne et l'abandonne aux Semipelagiens passe aujourd'hui pour la plus commune parmi les savans." [407]

It has been matter of question whether Vincentius is to be credited with the authorship of the "Objectiones Vincentianae," a collection of Sixteen Inferences alleged to be deducible from St. Augustine's writings, which has come down to us in Prosper's Reply.

Its date coincides so nearly with that of the Commonitory as to preclude all doubt as to the identity of authorship on that score, [408] and it must be confessed that its animus and that of the 70th and 86th sections of the Commonitory are too much in keeping to make it difficult to believe that both are from the same pen.

Vincentius's object in the following treatise is to provide himself, as he states, with a general rule whereby to distinguish Catholic truth from heresy; and he commits what he has learnt, he adds, to writing, that he may have it by him for reference as a Commonitory, or Remembrancer, to refresh his memory.

This rule, in brief, is the authority of Holy Scripture. By that all questions must be tried in the first instance. And it would be abundantly sufficient, but that, unfortunately, men differ in the interpretation of Holy Scripture. The rule, therefore, must be supplemented by an appeal to that sense of Holy Scripture which is supported by universality, antiquity, and consent: by universality, when it is the faith of the whole Church; by antiquity, when it is that which has been held from the earliest times; by consent, when it has been the acknowledged belief of all, or of almost all, whose office and character gave authority to their determinations. This is the famous "Quod ubique, quod semper, quod ab omnibus," with which Vincentius's name is associated. [409] The body of the work is taken up with its illustration and application.

The work consisted originally of two books; but unfortunately the second was lost, or rather, as Gennadius says, was stolen, while the author was still alive; and there remains to us nothing but a recapitulation of its contents, which the author, unwilling to encounter the labour of rewriting the whole, has drawn up. [410]

In prosecution of his purpose Vincentius proceeds to show how his rule applies for the detection of error in the instances of some of the more notorious heretics and schismatics who up to his time had made havoc of the Church,--the Donatists and the Arians, for instance, and the maintainers of the iteration of Baptism; and how the great defenders of the Faith were guided in their maintenance of the truth by its observance. [411]

But the perplexing question occurs: Wherefore, in God's providence, were persons, eminent for their attainments and their piety, such as Photinus, Apollinaris, and

Nestorius, permitted to fall into heresy? [412] To which the answer is, For the Church's trial. And Vincentius proceeds to show, in the case of each of these, how great a trial to the Church his fall was. This leads him to give an account of their erroneous teaching severally, [413] from which he turns aside for a while to expound the Catholic doctrine of the Trinity as opposed to the heresy of Photinus, and of the Incarnation as opposed to the heresies of Apollinaris and Nestorius, in an exposition remarkable for its clearness and precision. [414] It contains so much in common with the so-called Athanasian Creed, both as to the sentiments and the language, that some have inferred from it, that Vincentius was the author of that Formulary. [415]

Returning from this digression, Vincentius proceeds, after promising to deal with these subjects more fully on a future occasion, [416] to two other very signal instances of heretical defection caused by the disregard of antiquity and universality; those of Origen [417] and Tertullian, [418] of both of whom he draws a vivid picture, contrasting them, such as they were before their fall with what they became afterwards, and enlarging on the grievous injury to the Church generally, and the distressing trial to individuals in particular, consequent upon their defection.

But it will be asked, Is Christian doctrine to remain at a standstill? Is there to be no progress, as in other sciences? [419] Undoubtedly there is to be progress; but it must be real progress, analogous, for instance, to the growth of the human body from infancy to childhood, from childhood to mature age; or to the development of a plant from the seed to the full-grown vegetable or tree; it must be such as the elucidation of what was before obscure, the following out into detail of what was before expressed only in general terms, [420] not the addition of new doctrine, not the rejection of old.

One difficulty which is not unlikely to perplex a simple Christian is the readiness with which heretics appeal to Scripture, following therein the example of their arch-leader, who, in his temptation of our Lord, dared to make use of arms drawn from that armoury. [421] This leads to the question, How are we to ascertain the true sense of Scripture? And, in the answer to it, to a more detailed exposition of the general rule given at the outset.

Scripture, then, must be interpreted in accordance with the tradition of the Catholic Church, our guide being antiquity, universality, consent.

With regard to antiquity, that interpretation must be held to which has been handed down from the earliest times; with regard to universality, that which has always been held, if not by all, at least by the most part, in preference to that which has been held only by a few; with regard to consent, the determination of a General Council on any point will of course be of summary authority, and will hold the first place; next to this, the interpretation which has been held uniformly and persistently by all those

Fathers, or by a majority of them, who have lived and died in the communion of the Catholic Church. Accordingly, whatsoever interpretation of Holy Scripture is opposed to an interpretation thus authenticated, even though supported by the authority of one or another individual teacher, however eminent, whether by his position, or his attainments, or his piety, or by all of these together, must be rejected as novel and unsound.

Here the first Commonitory ends; but it ends with a promise of a still further and more detailed inquiry, to be prosecuted in the Commonitory which is to follow, into the way in which the opinions of the ancient Fathers are to be collected, and the rule of faith determined in accordance with them.

Unfortunately that promise, however fulfilled according to the author's intention, has been frustrated to his readers. The second Commonitory, as was said above, was lost, or rather stolen, and all that remains to us is a brief and apparently partial recapitulation of its contents and of the contents of the preceding.

In this Vincentius repeats the rule for ascertaining the Catholic doctrine which he had laid down at the outset, enlarging especially upon the way in which the consent of the Fathers is to be arrived at, and illustrating what he says by the course pursued by the Council of Ephesus in the matter of Nestorius,--how the Fathers of the Council, instead of resting upon their own judgment, eminent as many of them were, collected together the opinions of the most illustrious of their predecessors, and following their consentient belief, determined the question before them. To this most noteworthy example he adds the authority of two bishops of Rome, Sixtus III., then occupying the Papal Chair, and Celestine, his immediate predecessor,--the gist of the whole being the confirmation of the rule which it had been his object to enforce throughout the Treatise--that profane novelties must be rejected, and that faith alone adhered to which the universal Church has held consentiently from the earliest times, Quod ubique, quod semper, quod ab omnibus.

[398] De Scriptoribus Ecclesiasticis. Gennadius's work is to be found at the end of the second volume of Vallarsius's edition of St. Jerome's works.

[399] Now St. Honorat, so called from St. Honoratus, the founder of the monastery. The monastery seems at first to have consisted of an aggregation of separate cells, each of which, according to the usage of that time, would be called a "monasterium." "Tota ubique insula, exstructis cellulis, unum velut monasterium evasit."-- Cardinal Noris, Histor. Pelag. p. 251. "Monasterium potest unius monachi habitaculum nominari."--Cassian. Collat. xvii. 18. Among its more prominent members, contemporary with Vincentius, were Honoratus and Hilary, afterwards successively bishops of Arles, and Faustus, afterwards bishop of Riez, all of them in sympathy with the neighbouring clergy of Marseilles, opposed to St. Augustine's later teaching, and holding

what was afterwards called Semipelagian doctrine. The adjoining islet of St. Marguerite, one of the Lerins group, has acquired notoriety of late, from having been the place to which Marshal Bazaine, the betrayer of Metz, was banished in 1873.

[400] S: 79.

[401] S: 80.

[402] S: 85.

[403] De Illustr. Eccles. Scrip. c. 84.

[404] xv. p. 146.

[405] Cardinal Noris does not hesitate to say of him, "Non modo Semipelagianum se prodit, sed disertis verbis Augustini discipulos tanquam haereticos traducit."--Historia Pelagiana, p. 245. See below, Appendix II.

[406] See Prosper's letter to Augustine in Augustine's works, Ep. 225, Tom. ii. Ed. Paris, 1836, etc.

[407] T. xv. p. 146.

[408] The Objectiones Vincentianae must have been published at some time between the publication of St. Augustine's Antipelagian Treatises and the death of Prosper. They are to be found in Prosper's Reply, contained in St. Augustine's works, Appendix, Tom. x. coll. 2535. et seq. Paris, 1836, etc.

[409] S: 6.

[410] S:S: 77-88.

[411] S:S: 9 sqq.

[412] S:S: 27 sqq.

[413] S:S: 32 sqq.

[414] S:S: 36 sqq.

[415] Antelmi, Nova de Symbolo Athanasiano Disquisitio. See the note on S: 42, Appendix I.

[416] S: 42.

[417] S:S: 44-46.

[418] S: 47.

[419] S: 55.

[420] S:S: 55-60. For instances in point, he might have referred to the enlargement and expansion of the earlier Creed, first in the Nicene, afterward in the Constantinopolitan Formulary. Thus, in the Definition of the Faith of the Council of Chalcedon, the Fathers are careful to explain that they are making no addition to the original deposit, but amply unfolding and rendering more intelligible what before had been less distinctly set forth: "Teaching in its fulness the doctrine which from the beginning hath remained unshaken, it decrees, in the

first place that the Creed of the 318 (the original Nicene Creed) remain untouched; and on account of those who impugn the Holy Spirit, it ratifies and confirms the doctrine subsequently delivered, concerning the essence of the Holy Spirit, by the hundred and fifty holy Fathers, (the Constantinopolitan Creed), which they promulgated for universal acceptance, not as though they were supplying some omission of their predecessors, but testifying in express words in writing their own minds concerning the Holy Spirit."

[421] S:S: 65 sqq.

A Commonitory [422]
For the Antiquity and Universality of the Catholic Faith Against the Profane Novelties of All Heresies.

Chapter I.
The Object of the Following Treatise.

[1.] I, Peregrinus, [423] who am the least of all the servants of God, remembering the admonition of Scripture, "Ask thy fathers and they will tell thee, thine elders and they will declare unto thee," [424] and again, "Bow down thine ear to the words of the wise," [425] and once more, "My son, forget not these instructions, but let thy heart keep my words:" [426] remembering these admonitions, I say, I, Peregrinus, am persuaded, that, the Lord helping me, it will be of no little use and certainly as regards my own feeble powers, it is most necessary, that I should put down in writing the things which I have truthfully received from the holy Fathers, since I shall then have ready at hand wherewith by constant reading to make amends for the weakness of my memory.

[2.] To this I am incited not only by regard to the fruit to be expected from my labour but also by the consideration of time and the opportuneness of place:

By the consideration of time,--for seeing that time seizes upon all things human, we also in turn ought to snatch from it something which may profit us to eternal life, especially since a certain awful expectation of the approach of the divine judgment importunately demands increased earnestness in religion, while the subtle craftiness of new heretics calls for no ordinary care and attention.

I am incited also by the opportuneness of place, in that, avoiding the concourse and crowds of cities, I am dwelling in the seclusion of a Monastery, situated in a remote grange, [427] where, I can follow without distraction the Psalmist's [428] admonition, "Be still, and know that I am God."

Moreover, it suits well with my purpose in adopting this life; for, whereas I was at one time involved in the manifold and deplorable tempests of secular warfare, I have now at length, under Christ's auspices, cast anchor in the harbour of religion, a harbour to all always most safe, in order that, having there been freed from the blasts of vanity and pride, and propitiating God by the sacrifice of Christian humility, I may be able to escape not only the shipwrecks of the present life, but also the flames of the world to come.

[3.] But now, in the Lord's name, I will set about the object I have in view; that is to say, to record with the fidelity of a narrator rather than the presumption of an author, the things which our forefathers have handed down to us and committed to our keeping, yet observing this rule in what I write, that I shall by no means touch upon everything that might be said, but only upon what is necessary; nor yet in an ornate and exact style, but in simple and ordinary language, [429] so that the most part may seem to be intimated, rather than set forth in detail. Let those cultivate elegance and exactness who are confident of their ability or are moved by a sense of duty. For me it will be enough to have provided a Commonitory (or Remembrancer) for myself, such as may aid my memory, or rather, provide against my forgetfulness: which same Commonitory however, I shall endeavor, the Lord helping me, to amend and make more complete by little and little, day by day, by recalling to mind what I have learnt. I mention this at the outset, that if by chance what I write should slip out of my possession and come into the hands of holy men, they may forbear to blame anything therein hastily, when they see that there is a promise that it will yet be amended and made more complete.

[422] Commonitory. I have retained the original title in its anglicised form, already familiar to English ears in connection with the name of Vincentius. Its meaning as he uses it is indicated sufficiently, in S: 3, "An aid to memory." Technically, it meant a Paper of Instructions given to a person charged with a commission, to assist his memory as to its details.

[423] Peregrinus. It does not appear why Vincentius writes under an assumed name. Vossius, with whom

Cardinal Noris evidently agrees, supposes that his object was to avoid openly avowing himself the author of a work which covertly attacked St. Augustine. Vossius, Histor. Pelag. p. 246. Ego quidem ad Vossii sententiam plane accessissem, nisi tot delatae a sapientissimis Scriptoribus Commonitorio laudes religionem mihi pene injecissent.--Noris, Histor. Pelag. p. 246.

[424] Deut. xxxii. 7.

[425] Prov. xxii. 17.

[426] Prov. iii. 1.

[427] Noris, from this word, "villula," a grange or country house, concludes that Vincentius, at the time of writing, though a monk, was not a monk of Lerins for there could be no "villula" there then, Honoratus having found the island desolate and without inhabitant, when he settled on it but a few years previously, "vacantem insulam ob nimictatem squaloris, et inaccessam venenatorum animalium metu." Histor. Pelag. p. 251. Why, however, may not the "villula" have been built subsequently to Honoratus's settlement and indeed, as a part of it? Whether Vincentius was an inmate of the monastery of Lerins at the time of writing the Commonitory or not, he was so eventually, and died there.

[428] Ps. xlvi. 10.

[429] "Il dit qu'il l'a voulu ecrire d'un style facile et commun, sans le vouloir orner et polir; et je voudrois que les ouvrages qu'on a pris le plus de peine `a polir dans ce siecle (le 4me) et dans le suivant, ressemblassent `a celui-ci." Tillemont, T. xv. p. 144.

Chapter II.
A General Rule for distinguishing the Truth of the Catholic Faith from the Falsehood of Heretical Pravity.

[4.] I have often then inquired earnestly and attentively of very many men eminent for sanctity and learning, how and by what sure and so to speak universal rule I may be able to distinguish the truth of Catholic faith from the falsehood of heretical pravity; and I have always, and in almost every instance, received an answer to this effect: That whether I or any one else should wish to detect the frauds and avoid the snares of heretics as they rise, and to continue sound and complete in the Catholic faith, we must, the Lord helping, fortify our own belief in two ways; first, by the authority of the Divine Law, and then, by the Tradition of the Catholic Church.

[5.] But here some one perhaps will ask, Since the canon of Scripture is complete, and sufficient of itself for everything, and more than sufficient, what need is there to join with it the authority of the Church's interpretation? For this reason,--because, owing to the depth of Holy Scripture, all do not accept it in one and the same sense, but one understands its words in one way, another in another; so that it seems to be capable of as many interpretations as there are interpreters. For Novatian expounds it one way, Sabellius another,

Donatus another, Arius, Eunomius, Macedonius, another, Photinus, Apollinaris, Priscillian, another, Iovinian, Pelagius, Celestius, another, lastly, Nestorius another. Therefore, it is very necessary, on account of so great intricacies of such various error, that the rule for the right understanding of the prophets and apostles should be framed in accordance with the standard of Ecclesiastical and Catholic interpretation.

[6.] Moreover, in the Catholic Church itself, all possible care must be taken, that we hold that faith which has been believed everywhere, always, by all. For that is truly and in the strictest sense "Catholic," which, as the name itself and the reason of the thing declare, comprehends all universally. This rule we shall observe if we follow universality, antiquity, consent. We shall follow universality if we confess that one faith to be true, which the whole Church throughout the world confesses; antiquity, if we in no wise depart from those interpretations which it is manifest were notoriously held by our holy ancestors and fathers; consent, in like manner, if in antiquity itself we adhere to the consentient definitions and determinations of all, or at the least of almost all priests and doctors.

Chapter III.
What is to be done if one or more dissent from the rest.

[7.] What then will a Catholic Christian do, if a small portion of the Church have cut itself off from the communion of the universal faith? What, surely, but prefer the soundness of the whole body to the unsoundness of a pestilent and corrupt member? What, if some novel contagion seek to infect not merely an insignificant portion of the Church, but the whole? Then it will be his care to cleave to antiquity, which at this day cannot possibly be seduced by any fraud of novelty.

[8.] But what, if in antiquity itself there be found error on the part of two or three men, or at any rate of a city or even of a province? Then it will be his care by all means, to prefer the decrees, if such there be, of an ancient General Council to the rashness and ignorance of a few. But what, if some error should spring up on which no such decree is found to bear? Then he must collate and consult and interrogate the opinions of the ancients, of those, namely, who, though living in divers times and places, yet continuing in the communion and faith of the one Catholic Church, stand forth acknowledged and approved authorities: and whatsoever he shall ascertain to have been held, written, taught, not by one or two of these only, but by all, equally, with one consent, openly, frequently, persistently, that he must understand that he himself also is to believe without any doubt or hesitation.

Chapter IV.
The evil resulting from the bringing in of Novel Doctrine shown in the instances of the Donatists and Arians.

[9.] But that we may make what we say more intelligible, we must illustrate it by individual examples, and enlarge upon it somewhat more fully, lest by aiming at too great brevity important matters be hurried over and lost sight of.

In the time of Donatus, [430] from whom his followers were called Donatists, when great numbers in Africa were rushing headlong into their own mad error, and unmindful of their name, their religion, their profession, were preferring the sacrilegious temerity of one man before the Church of Christ, then they alone throughout Africa were safe within the sacred precincts of the Catholic faith, who, detesting the profane schism, continued in communion with the universal Church, leaving to posterity an illustrious example, how, and how well in future the soundness of the whole body should be preferred before the madness of one, or at most of a few.

[10.] So also when the Arian poison had infected not an insignificant portion of the Church but almost the whole world, [431] so that a sort of blindness had fallen upon almost all the bishops [432] of the Latin tongue, circumvented partly by force partly by fraud, and was preventing them from seeing what was most expedient to be done in the midst of so much confusion, then whoever was a true lover and worshipper of Christ, preferring the ancient belief to the novel misbelief, escaped the pestilent infection.

[11.] By the peril of which time was abundantly shown how great a calamity the introduction of a novel doctrine causes. For then truly not only interests of small account, but others of the very gravest importance, were subverted. For not only affinities, relationships, friendships, families, but moreover, cities, peoples, provinces, nations, at last the whole Roman Empire, were shaken to their foundation and ruined. For when this same profane Arian novelty, like a Bellona or a Fury, had first taken captive the Emperor, [433] and had then subjected all the principal persons of the palace to new laws, from that time it never ceased to involve everything in confusion, disturbing all things, public and private, sacred and profane, paying no regard to what was good and true, but, as though holding a position of authority, smiting whomsoever it pleased. Then wives were violated, widows ravished, virgins profaned, monasteries demolished, clergymen ejected, the inferior clergy scourged, priests driven into exile, jails, prisons, mines, filled with saints, of whom the greater part, forbidden to enter into cities, thrust forth from their homes to wander in deserts and caves, among rocks and the haunts of wild beasts, exposed to nakedness, hunger, thirst, were worn out and consumed. Of all of which was there any other cause than that, while human superstitions are being brought in to supplant heavenly doctrine, while well established antiquity is being subverted by wicked novelty, while the institutions of former ages are being set at naught, while the decrees of our fathers are being rescinded, while the determinations of our ancestors are being torn in pieces, the lust of profane and novel curiosity refuses to restrict itself within the most chaste limits of hallowed and uncorrupt antiquity? [434]

[430] There were two persons of this name, both intimately connected with the schism,--the earlier one, bishop of Casa Nigra in Numidia, the other the successor of Majorinus, whom in the year 311 the party had elected to be bishop of Carthage in opposition to Cecilian, the Catholic bishop, the ground of the opposition being that the principal among Cecilian's consecrators lay under the charge of having delivered up the sacred books to the heathen magistrates in the Dioclesian persecution, and of having thereby rendered his ministerial acts invalid. It was from the last-mentioned probably that the sect was called. The Donatists affected great strictness of life, and ignoring the plain declarations of Scripture, and notably the prophetic representations contained in our Lord's parables of the Tares, the Draw-net, and others, they held that no church could be a true church which endured the presence of evil men in its society.

Accordingly they broke off communion with the rest of the African Church and with all who held communion with it, which was in effect the rest of Christendom, denying the validity of their sacraments, rebaptizing those who came over to them from other Christian bodies, and reordaining their clergy. The sect became so powerful that for some time it formed the stronger party in the church of North Western Africa, its bishops exceeding four hundred in number; but partly checked through the exertions of Augustine in the first years of the fifth century, and of Pope Gregory the Great at the close of the sixth, and partly weakened by divisions among themselves, they dwindled away and become extinct.

[431] The rise of Arianism was nearly contemporaneous with that of Donatism. It originated with Arius, a presbyter of Alexandria, a man of a subtle wit and a fluent tongue. He began by calling in question the teaching of his bishop, when discoursing on a certain occasion on the subject of the Trinity. For himself he denied our blessed Lord's coeternity and consubstantiality with the Father, which was in effect to deny that He is God in any true sense, though he made no scruple of giving Him the name. His doctrine may be best inferred from the anathema directed against it, appended to the original Nicene Creed: "Those who say, that once the Son of God did not exist, and that before He was begotten He did not exist, or who affirm that He is of a different substance or essence (from that of the

Father), or that His nature is mutable or alterable, those the Catholic and Apostolic Church anathematises." Arianism spread with great rapidity, and though condemned by the Council of Nicaea in 325, it gained fresh strength on the death of Constantine and the accession of Constantius, so that for many years thenceforward the history of the Church is occupied with nothing so much as with accounts of its struggle for supremacy. "Arians and Donatists began both about one time, which heresies, according to the different strength of their own sinews, wrought, as the hope of success led them, the one with the choicest wits, the other with the multitude, so far, that after long and troublesome experience, the perfectest view that men could take of both was hardly able to induce any certain determinate resolution, whether error may do more by the curious subtlety of sharp discourse, or else by the mere appearance of zeal and devout affection."--Hooker, Eccles. Pol. v. 62. S: 8.

[432] The Catholic bishops, in number more than four hundred, who at Ariminum, in 359, after having subscribed the Creed of Nicaea, were induced, partly by fraud, partly by threats, to repudiate its crucial terms and sign an Arian Formulary. It was in reference to this that St. Jerome wrote, "Ingemuit orbis, et Arium se esse miratus est." "The world groaned and marvelled to find itself Arian." He continues, "The vessel of the apostles was in extreme danger. The storm raged, the waves beat upon the ship, all hope was gone. The Lord awakes,

rebukes the tempest, the monster (Constantius) dies, tranquillity is restored. The bishops who had been thrust out from their sees return, through the clemency of the new emperor. Then did Egypt receive Athanasius in triumph, then did the Church of Gaul receive Hilary returning from battle, then did Italy put off her mourning garments at the return of Eusebius (of Vercellae)."--Advers. Luciferianos, S: 10.

[433] Constantius, the Emperor of the West.

[434] Though Vincentius' account of the Arian persecutions refers to those under Arian emperors, Constantius and Valens, the former especially, yet he could not but have had in mind the atrocious cruelties which were being perpetrated, at the time when he was writing, by the Arian Vandals in Africa. Possidius, in his life of St. Augustine, who lay on his death-bed in Hippo while the fierce Vandal host was encamped round the city (c. xxviii.), gives a detailed account of them belonging to a date some four years earlier, entirely of a piece with Vincentius' description in the text. Victor, bishop of Vite, himself a sufferer, has left a still ampler relation, De Persecutione Vandalorum.

Chapter V.
The Example set us by the Martyrs, whom no force could hinder from defending the Faith of their Predecessors.

[12.] But it may be, we invent these charges out of hatred to novelty and zeal for antiquity. Whoever is disposed to listen to such an insinuation, let him at least believe the blessed Ambrose, who, deploring the acerbity of the time, says, in the second book of his work addressed to the Emperor Gratian: [435] "Enough now, O God Almighty! have we expiated with our own ruin, with our own blood, the slaughter of Confessors, the banishment of priests, and the wickedness of such extreme impiety. It is clear, beyond question, that they who have violated the faith cannot remain in safety."

And again in the third book of the same work, [436] "Let us observe the precepts of our predecessors, and not transgress with rude rashness the landmarks which we have inherited from them. That sealed Book of Prophecy no Elders, no Powers, no Angels, no Archangels, dared to open. To Christ alone was reserved the prerogative of explaining it. [437] Who of us may dare to unseal the Sacerdotal Book sealed by Confessors, and consecrated already by the martyrdom of numbers, which they who had been compelled by force to unseal afterwards resealed, condemning the fraud which had been practised upon them; while they who had not

ventured to tamper with it proved themselves
Confessors and martyrs? How can we deny the faith of
those whose victory we proclaim?"

[13.] We proclaim it truly, O venerable Ambrose, we
proclaim it, and applaud and admire. For who is there so
demented, who, though not able to overtake, does not at
least earnestly desire to follow those whom no force
could deter from defending the faith of their ancestors,
no threats, no blandishments, not life, not death, not the
palace, not the Imperial Guards, not the Emperor, not
the empire itself, not men, not demons?--whom, I say, as
a recompense for their steadfastness in adhering to
religious antiquity, the Lord counted worthy of so great a
reward, that by their instrumentality He restored
churches which had been destroyed, quickened with new
life peoples who were spiritually dead, replaced on the
heads of priests the crowns which had been torn from
them, washed out those abominable, I will not say
letters, but blotches (non literas, sed lituras) of novel
impiety, with a fountain of believing tears, which God
opened in the hearts of the bishops?--lastly, when almost
the whole world was overwhelmed by a ruthless tempest
of unlooked for heresy, recalled it from novel misbelief
to the ancient faith, from the madness of novelty to the
soundness of antiquity, from the blindness of novelty to
pristine light?

[14.] But in this divine virtue, as we may call it, exhibited
by these Confessors, we must note especially that the
defence which they then undertook in appealing to the

Ancient Church, was the defence, not of a part, but of the whole body. For it was not right that men of such eminence should uphold with so huge an effort the vague and conflicting notions of one or two men, or should exert themselves in the defence of some ill-advised combination of some petty province; but adhering to the decrees and definitions of the universal priesthood of Holy Church, the heirs of Apostolic and Catholic truth, they chose rather to deliver up themselves than to betray the faith of universality and antiquity. For which cause they were deemed worthy of so great glory as not only to be accounted Confessors, but rightly, and deservedly to be accounted foremost among Confessors.

[435] St. Ambrose. De Fide, l. 2, c. 15, S: 141. See also St. Jerome adv. Luciferianos, S: 19.

[436] Ibid. l. 3, S: 128. St. Ambrose speaks of the Gothic war as a judgment upon Valens, both for his Arianism and for his persecution of the Catholics. He had permitted the Goths to cross the Danube, and settle in Thrace and the adjoining parts, with the understanding that they should embrace Christianity in its Arian form. They had now turned against him, and Gratian was on the eve of setting out to carry aid to him. St. Ambrose's book, De Fide, was written to confirm Gratian in the Catholic faith, in view especially of the Arian influence to which he might be subjected in his intercourse with Valens. Valens was killed the following year, 378, at the battle of Adrianople.

[437] Rev. v. 1-5.

Chapter VI.
The example of Pope Stephen in resisting the Iteration of Baptism.

[15.] Great then is the example of these same blessed men, an example plainly divine, and worthy to be called to mind, and meditated upon continually by every true Catholic, who, like the seven-branched candlestick, shining with the sevenfold light of the Holy Spirit, showed to posterity how thenceforward the audaciousness of profane novelty, in all the several rantings of error, might be crushed by the authority of hallowed antiquity.

Nor is there anything new in this? For it has always been the case in the Church, that the more a man is under the influence of religion, so much the more prompt is he to oppose innovations. Examples there are without number: but to be brief, we will take one, and that, in preference to others, from the Apostolic See, [438] so that it may be clearer than day to every one with how great energy, with how great zeal, with how great earnestness, the blessed successors of the blessed apostles have constantly defended the integrity of the religion which they have once received.

[16.] Once on a time then, Agrippinus, [439] bishop of Carthage, of venerable memory, held the doctrine--and he was the first who held it--that Baptism ought to be repeated, contrary to the divine canon, contrary to the rule of the universal Church, contrary to the customs and institutions of our ancestors. This innovation drew after it such an amount of evil, that it not only gave an example of sacrilege to heretics of all sorts, but proved an occasion of error to certain Catholics even.

When then all men protested against the novelty, and the priesthood everywhere, each as his zeal prompted him, opposed it, Pope Stephen of blessed memory, Prelate of the Apostolic See, in conjunction indeed with his colleagues but yet himself the foremost, withstood it, thinking it right, I doubt not, that as he exceeded all others in the authority of his place, so he should also in the devotion of his faith. In fine, in an epistle sent at the time to Africa, he laid down this rule: "Let there be no innovation--nothing but what has been handed down." [440] For that holy and prudent man well knew that true piety admits no other rule than that whatsoever things have been faithfully received from our fathers the same are to be faithfully consigned to our children; and that it is our duty, not to lead religion whither we would, but rather to follow religion whither it leads; and that it is the part of Christian modesty and gravity not to hand down our own beliefs or observances to those who come after us, but to preserve and keep what we have received from those who went before us. What then was the issue of the whole matter? What but the usual and customary one? Antiquity was retained, novelty was rejected.

[17.] But it may be, the cause of innovation at that time lacked patronage. On the contrary, it had in its favor such powerful talent, such copious eloquence, such a number of partisans, so much resemblance to truth, such weighty support in Scripture (only interpreted in a novel and perverse sense), that it seems to me that that whole conspiracy could not possibly have been defeated, unless the sole cause of this extraordinary stir, the very novelty of what was so undertaken, so defended, so belauded, had proved wanting to it. In the end, what result, under God, had that same African Council or decree? [441] None whatever. The whole affair, as though a dream, a fable, a thing of no possible account, was annulled, cancelled, and trodden underfoot.

[18.] And O marvellous revolution! The authors of this same doctrine are judged Catholics, the followers heretics; the teachers are absolved, the disciples condemned; the writers of the books will be children of the Kingdom, the defenders of them will have their portion in Hell. For who is so demented as to doubt that that blessed light among all holy bishops and martyrs, Cyprian, together with the rest of his colleagues, will reign with Christ; or, who on the other hand so sacrilegious as to deny that the Donatists and those other pests, who boast the authority of that council for their iteration of baptism, will be consigned to eternal fire with the devil? [442]

[438] "The Apostolic see" (Sedes Apostolica) here means Rome of course. But the title was not restricted to

Rome. It was common to all sees which could claim an apostle as their Founder. Thus St. Augustine, suggesting a rule for determining what books are to be regarded as Canonical, says, "In Canonicis Scripturis Ecclesiarum Catholicarum quamplurium auctoritatem sequatur, inter quas sane illae sint quae Apostolicas Sedes habere et Epistolas accipere meruerunt." "Let him follow the authority of those Catholic Churches which have been counted worthy to have Apostolic Sees; i.e., to have been founded by Apostles, and to have been the recipients of Apostolic Epistles."--De Doctr. Christiana, II. S: 13. But the title, even in St. Augustine's time, had even a wider meaning. "Anciently every bishop's see was dignified with the title of Sedes Apostolica, which in those days was no peculiar title of the bishop of Rome, but given to all bishops in general, as deriving their origin and counting their succession from the apostles."--Bingham, Antiq. II., c. 2, S: 3.

[439] Agrippinus. See note 4, below.

[440] Stephen's letter has not come down to us, happily perhaps for his credit, judging by the terms in which Cyprian speaks of it in the letter in which he quotes the passage in the text.--Ad Pompeian, Ep. 74.

[441] The Council held under the presidency of Cyprian in 256. Its acts are contained in Cyprian's works, Ed. Fell. pp. 158, etc. An earlier council had been held in the same city in the beginning of the century under Agrippinus. Both had affirmed the necessity of

rebaptizing heretics, or, as they would rather have said, of baptizing them. The controversy was set at rest by a decision of the council of Arles, in 314, which ordered, in its Eighth Canon, that if the baptism had been administered in the name of the Trinity, converts should be admitted simply by the imposition of hands that they might receive the Holy Ghost.

[442] See Hooker's reference to this passage.--Eccles. Poll. v. 62, S: 9.

Chapter VII.
How Heretics, craftily cite obscure passages in ancient writers in support of their own novelties.

[19.] This condemnation, indeed, [443] seems to have been providentially promulgated as though with a special view to the fraud of those who, contriving to dress up a heresy under a name other than its own, get hold often of the works of some ancient writer, not very clearly expressed, which, owing to the very obscurity of their own doctrine, have the appearance of agreeing with it, so that they get the credit of being neither the first nor the only persons who have held it. This wickedness of theirs, in my judgment, is doubly hateful: first, because they are not afraid to invite others to drink of the poison of heresy; and secondly, because with profane breath, as though fanning smouldering embers into flame, they blow upon the memory of each holy man, and spread an evil report of what ought to be buried in silence by bringing it again under notice, thus treading in the footsteps of their father Ham, who not only forebore to cover the nakedness of the venerable Noah, but told it to the others that they might laugh at it, offending thereby so grievously against the duty of filial piety, that even his descendants were involved with him in the curse which he drew down, widely differing from those blessed brothers of his, who would neither pollute their own eyes by looking upon the nakedness of their revered father, nor would suffer others to do so, but went backwards, as the Scripture says, and covered him, that is, they neither approved nor betrayed the fault of the holy man, for which cause they were rewarded with a benediction on themselves and their posterity. [444]

[20.] But to return to the matter in hand: It behoves us then to have a great dread of the crime of perverting the faith and adulterating religion, a crime from which we are deterred not only by the Church's discipline, but also by the censure of apostolical authority. For every one knows how gravely, how severely, how vehemently, the blessed apostle Paul inveighs against certain, who, with marvellous levity, had "been so soon removed from him who had called them to the grace of Christ to another Gospel, which was not another;" [445] "who had heaped to themselves teachers after their own lusts, turning away their ears from the truth, and being turned aside unto fables;" [446] "having damnation because they had cast off their first faith;" [447] who had been deceived by those of whom the same apostle writes to the Roman Christians, "Now, I beseech you, brethren, mark them which cause divisions and offences, contrary to the doctrine which ye have learned, and avoid them. For they that are such serve not the Lord Christ, but their own belly, and by good words and fair speeches deceive the hearts of the simple," [448] "who enter into houses, and lead captive silly women laden with sins, led away with diverse lusts, ever learning and never able to come to the knowledge of the truth;" [449] "vain talkers and deceivers, who subvert whole houses, teaching things

which they ought not, for filthy lucre's sake;" [450] "men
of corrupt minds, reprobate concerning the faith;" [451]
"proud knowing nothing, but doting about questions
and strifes of words, destitute of the truth, supposing
that godliness is gain," [452] "withal learning to be idle,
wandering about from house to house, and not only idle,
but tattlers also and busy-bodies, speaking things which
they ought not," [453] "who having put away a good
conscience have made shipwreck concerning the faith;"
[454] "whose profane and vain babblings increase unto
more ungodliness, and their word doth eat as doth a
cancer." [455] Well, also, is it written of them: "But they
shall proceed no further: for their folly shall be manifest
unto all men, as theirs also was." [456]

[443] The condemnation of St. Cyprian's practice of
rebaptism.

[444] Gen. ix. 22.

[445] Gal. i. 6.

[446] 2 Tim. iv. 3, 4.

[447] 1 Tim. v. 12.

[448] Rom. xvi. 17, 18.

[449] 2 Tim. iii. 6.

[450] Tit. i. 10.

[451] 2 Tim. iii. 8.

[452] 1 Tim. vi. 4.

[453] 1 Tim. v. 13.

[454] 1 Tim. i. 19.

[455] 2 Tim. ii. 16, 17.

[456] 2 Tim. iii. 9.

Chapter VIII.
Exposition of St. Paul's Words, Gal. i. 8.

[21.] When therefore certain of this sort wandering about provinces and cities, and carrying with them their venal errors, had found their way to Galatia, and when the Galatians, on hearing them, nauseating the truth, and vomiting up the manna of Apostolic and Catholic doctrine, were delighted with the garbage of heretical novelty, the apostle putting in exercise the authority of his office, delivered his sentence with the utmost severity, "Though we," he says, "or an angel from heaven, preach any other Gospel unto you than that which we have preached unto you, let him be accursed." [457]

[22.] Why does he say "Though we"? why not rather "though I"? He means, "though Peter, though Andrew, though John, in a word, though the whole company of apostles, preach unto you other than we have preached unto you, let him be accursed." Tremendous severity! He spares neither himself nor his fellow apostles, so he may preserve unaltered the faith which was at first delivered. Nay, this is not all. He goes on "Even though an angel from heaven preach unto you any other Gospel than that which we have preached unto you, let him be accursed." It was not enough for the preservation of the faith once delivered to have referred to man; he must needs comprehend angels also. "Though we," he says, "or an angel from heaven." Not that the holy angels of heaven are now capable of sinning. But what he means is: Even if that were to happen which cannot happen,--if any one, be he who he may, attempt to alter the faith once for all delivered, let him be accursed.

[23.] But it may be, he spoke thus in the first instance inconsiderately, giving vent to human impetuosity rather than expressing himself under divine guidance. Far from it. He follows up what he had said, and urges it with intense reiterated earnestness, "As we said before, so say I now again, If any man preach any other Gospel to you than that ye have received, let him be accursed." He does not say, "If any man deliver to you another message than that you have received, let him be blessed, praised, welcomed,"--no; but "let him be accursed," [anathema] i.e., separated, segregated, excluded, lest the dire contagion of a single sheep contaminate the guiltless flock of Christ by his poisonous intermixture with them.

[457] Gal. i. 8.

Chapter IX.
His warning to the Galatians a warning to all.

[24.] But, possibly, this warning was intended for the Galatians only. Be it so; then those other exhortations which follow in the same Epistle were intended for the Galatians only, such as, "If we live in the Spirit, let us also walk in the Spirit; let us not be desirous of vain glory, provoking one another, envying one another," etc.; [458] which alternative if it be absurd, and the injunctions were meant equally for all, then it follows, that as these injunctions which relate to morals, so those warnings which relate to faith are meant equally for all; and just as it is unlawful for all to provoke one another, or to envy one another, so, likewise, it is unlawful for all to receive any other Gospel than that which the Catholic Church preaches everywhere.

[25.] Or perhaps the anathema pronounced on any one who should preach another Gospel than that which had been preached was meant for those times, not for the present. Then, also, the exhortation, "Walk in the Spirit and ye shall not fulfil the lust of the flesh," [459] was meant for those times, not for the present. But if it be both impious and pernicious to believe this, then it follows necessarily, that as these injunctions are to be observed by all ages, so those warnings also which forbid alteration of the faith are warnings intended for all ages. To preach any doctrine therefore to Catholic

Christians other than what they have received never was lawful, never is lawful, never will be lawful: and to anathematize those who preach anything other than what has once been received, always was a duty, always is a duty, always will be a duty.

[26.] Which being the case, is there any one either so audacious as to preach any other doctrine than that which the Church preaches, or so inconstant as to receive any other doctrine than that which he has received from the Church? That elect vessel, that teacher of the Gentiles, that trumpet of the apostles, that preacher whose commission was to the whole earth, that man who was caught up to heaven, [460] cries and cries again in his Epistles to all, always, in all places, "If any man preach any new doctrine, let him be accursed." On the other hand, an ephemeral, moribund set of frogs, fleas, and flies, such as the Pelagians, call out in opposition, and that to Catholics, "Take our word, follow our lead, accept our exposition, condemn what you used to hold, hold what you used to condemn, cast aside the ancient faith, the institutes of your fathers, the trusts left for you by your ancestors and receive instead,--what? I tremble to utter it: for it is so full of arrogance and self-conceit, that it seems to me that not only to affirm it, but even to refute it, cannot be done without guilt in some sort.

[458] Gal. v. 25.

[459] Gal. v. 16.

[460] 2 Cor. xii. 2.

Chapter X.
Why Eminent Men are permitted by God to become Authors of Novelties in the Church.

[27.] But some one will ask, How is it then, that certain excellent persons, and of position in the Church, are often permitted by God to preach novel doctrines to Catholics? A proper question, certainly, and one which ought to be very carefully and fully dealt with, but answered at the same time, not in reliance upon one's own ability, but by the authority of the divine Law, and by appeal to the Church's determination.

Let us listen, then, to Holy Moses, and let him teach us why learned men, and such as because of their knowledge are even called Prophets by the apostle, are sometimes permitted to put forth novel doctrines, which the Old Testament is wont, by way of allegory, to call "strange gods," forasmuch as heretics pay the same sort of reverence to their notions that the Gentiles do to their gods.

[28.] Blessed Moses, then, writes thus in Deuteronomy: [461] "If there arise among you a prophet or a dreamer of dreams," that is, one holding office as a Doctor in the Church, who is believed by his disciples or auditors to teach by revelation: well,--what follows? "and giveth thee a sign or a wonder, and the sign or the wonder come to pass whereof he spake,"--he is pointing to some eminent doctor, whose learning is such that his followers believe him not only to know things human, but, moreover, to foreknow things superhuman, such as, their disciples commonly boast, were Valentinus, Donatus, Photinus, Apollinaris, and the rest of that sort! What next? "And shall say to thee, Let us go after other gods, whom thou knowest not, and serve them." What are those other gods but strange errors which thou knowest not, that is, new and such as were never heard of before? "And let us serve them;" that is, "Let us believe them, follow them." What last? "Thou shalt not hearken to the words of that prophet or dreamer of dreams." And why, I pray thee, does not God forbid to be taught what God forbids to be heard? "For the Lord, your God, trieth you, to know whether you love Him with all your heart and with all your soul." The reason is clearer than day why Divine Providence sometimes permits certain doctors of the Churches to preach new doctrines--"That the Lord your God may try you;" he says. And assuredly it is a great trial when one whom thou believest to be a prophet, a disciple of prophets, a doctor and defender of the truth, whom thou hast folded to thy breast with the utmost veneration and love, when such a one of a sudden secretly and furtively brings in noxious errors, which thou canst neither quickly detect, being held by the prestige of former authority, nor lightly think it right to condemn, being prevented by affection for thine old master.

[461] Deut. xiii. 1, etc.

Chapter XI.
Examples from Church History, confirming the words of Moses,--Nestorius, Photinus, Apollinaris.

[29.] Here, perhaps, some one will require us to illustrate the words of holy Moses by examples from Church History. The demand is a fair one, nor shall it wait long for satisfaction.

For to take first a very recent and very plain case: what sort of trial, think we, was that which the Church had experience of the other day, when that unhappy Nestorius, [462] all at once metamorphosed from a sheep into a wolf, began to make havoc of the flock of Christ, while as yet a large proportion of those whom he was devouring believed him to be a sheep, and consequently were the more exposed to his attacks? For who would readily suppose him to be in error, who was known to have been elected by the high choice of the Emperor, and to be held in the greatest esteem by the priesthood? who would readily suppose him to be in error, who, greatly beloved by the holy brethren, and in high favor with the populace, expounded the Scriptures in public daily, and confuted the pestilent errors both of Jews and Heathens? Who could choose but believe that his teaching was Orthodox, his preaching Orthodox, his belief Orthodox, who, that he might open the way to one heresy of his own, was zealously inveighing against the blasphemies of all heresies? But this was the very thing which Moses says: "The Lord your God doth try you that He may know whether you love Him or not."

[30.] Leaving Nestorius, in whom there was always more that men admired than they were profited by, more of show than of reality, whom natural ability, rather than divine grace, magnified, for a time in the opinion of the common people, let us pass on to speak of those who, being persons of great attainments and of much industry, proved no small trial to Catholics. Such, for instance, was Photinus, in Pannonia, [463] who, in the memory of our fathers, is said to have been a trial to the Church of Sirmium, where, when he had been raised to the priesthood with universal approbation, and had discharged the office for some time as a Catholic, all of a sudden, like that evil prophet or dreamer of dreams whom Moses refers to, he began to persuade the people whom God had intrusted, to his charge, to follow "strange gods," that is, strange errors, which before they knew not. But there was nothing unusual in this: the mischief of the matter was, that for the perpetration of so great wickedness he availed himself of no ordinary helps. For he was of great natural ability and of powerful eloquence, and had a wealth of learning, disputing and writing copiously and forcibly in both languages, as his books which remain, composed partly in Greek, partly in Latin, testify. But happily the sheep of Christ committed to him, vigilant and wary for the Catholic faith, quickly turned their eyes to the premonitory words of Moses, and, though admiring the eloquence of their prophet and

pastor, were not blind to the trial. For from
thenceforward they began to flee from him as a wolf,
whom formerly they had followed as the ram of the
flock.

[31.] Nor is it only in the instance of Photinus that we
learn the danger of this trial to the Church, and are
admonished withal of the need of double diligence in
guarding the faith. Apollinaris [464] holds out a like
warning. For he gave rise to great burning questions and
sore perplexities among his disciples, the Church's
authority drawing them one way, their Master's influence
the opposite; so that, wavering and tossed hither and
thither between the two, they were at a loss what course
to take.

But perhaps he was a person of no weight of character.
On the contrary, he was so eminent and so highly
esteemed that his word would only too readily be taken
on whatsoever subject. For what could exceed his
acuteness, his adroitness, his learning? How many
heresies did he, in many volumes, annihilate! How many
errors, hostile to the faith, did he confute! A proof of
which is that most noble and vast work, of not less than
thirty books, in which, with a great mass of arguments,
he repelled the insane calumnies of Porphyry. [465] It
would take a long time to enumerate all his works, which
assuredly would have placed him on a level with the very
chief of the Church's builders, if that profane lust of
heretical curiosity had not led him to devise I know not
what novelty which as though through the contagion of

a sort of leprosy both defiled all his labours, and caused his teachings to be pronounced the Church's trial instead of the Church's edification.

[462] Nestorius was a native of Germanicia, a town in the patriarchate of Antioch, of which Church he became a Presbyter. On the See of Constantinople becoming vacant by the death of Sisinnius, the Emperor Theodosius sent for him and caused him to be consecrated Archbishop. He was at first extremely popular, and so eloquent that people said of him (what was much to be said of a successor of Chrysostom), that there had never before been such a bishop. He was condemned by the Council of Ephesus, in 431. The emperor, after ordering him to return to the monastery to which he formally belonged, eventually banished him to the great Oasis, whence he was harried from place to place till death put an end to his sufferings, in 440. Evagrius, I. 7.

[463] Photinus, bishop of Sirmium in Pannonia, was a native of Galatia, and a disciple of Marcellus of Ancyra. Bishop Pearson (on the Creed, Art. 11) has an elaborate note, in which he collects together many notices of him left by the ancients. These agree with Vincentius in representing him as a man of extraordinary ability and of consummate eloquence. His heresy consisted in the denial of our blessed Lord's divine nature, whom he regarded as man, and nothing more, psilos anthropos, and as having had no existence before his birth of the Virgin. He was condemned in several synods, the fifth of

which, a Council of the Western bishops, held at Sirmium, in 350, deposed him. But in spite of the deposition, so great was his popularity, that he could not even yet be removed. The following year however he was by another council, held at the same place, again condemned, and sent into banishment. He died in Galatia in 377. See Cave, Hist. Lit., who refers with praise to a learned dissertation on Photinus by Larroque.

[464] Apollinaris the younger (a contemporary of Photinus), bishop of Laodicea in Syria, was one of the most distinguished men of the age in which he lived. Epiphanius (Haer. lxxvii. 2), referring to his fall into heresy, says that when it first began to be spoken of, people would hardly credit it, so great was the estimation in which he was held. His heresy, which consisted in the denial of the verity of our Lord's human nature, the Divine Word supplying the place of the rational soul, and in the assertion that his flesh was not derived from the Virgin, but was brought down from heaven, was condemned by the Council of Constantinople, in 381 (Canon I.). It was in reference to the latter form of it that the clause "of the Holy Ghost and the Virgin Mary" was inserted in the Nicene Creed.

[465] This work of which St. Jerome speaks in high terms (de Viris Illustr., c. 104), has not come down to us, nor indeed have his other writings, except in fragments.

Chapter XII.
A fuller account of the Errors of Photinus,
Apollinaris and Nestorius.

[32.] Here, possibly, I may be asked for some account of the above mentioned heresies; those, namely, of Nestorius, Apollinaris, and Photinus. This, indeed, does not belong to the matter in hand: for our object is not to enlarge upon the errors of individuals, but to produce instances of a few, in whom the applicability of Moses' words may be evidently and clearly seen; that is to say, that if at any time some Master in the Church, himself also a prophet in interpreting the mysteries of the prophets, should attempt to introduce some novel doctrine into the Church of God, Divine Providence permits this to happen in order to try us. It will be useful, therefore, by way of digression, to give a brief account of the opinions of the above-named heretics, Photinus, Apollinaris, Nestorius.

[33.] The heresy of Photinus, then, is as follows: He says that God is singular and sole, and is to be regarded as the Jews regarded Him. He denies the completeness of the Trinity, and does not believe that there is any Person of God the Word, or any Person of the Holy Ghost. Christ he affirms to be a mere man, whose original was from Mary. Hence he insists with the utmost obstinacy that we are to render worship only to the Person of God the Father, and that we are to honour Christ as man only. This is the doctrine of Photinus.

[34.] Apollinaris, affecting to agree with the Church as to the unity of the Trinity, though not this even with entire soundness of belief, [466] as to the Incarnation of the Lord, blasphemes openly. For he says that the flesh of our Saviour was either altogether devoid of a human soul, or, at all events, was devoid of a rational soul. Moreover, he says that this same flesh of the Lord was not received from the flesh of the holy Virgin Mary, but came down from heaven into the Virgin; and, ever wavering and undecided, he preaches one while that it was co-eternal with God the Word, another that it was made of the divine nature of the Word. For, denying that there are two substances in Christ, one divine, the other human, one from the Father, the other from his mother, he holds that the very nature of the Word was divided, as though one part of it remained in God, the other was converted into flesh: so that whereas the truth says that of two substances there is one Christ, he affirms, contrary to the truth, that of the one divinity of Christ there are become two substances. This, then, is the doctrine of Apollinaris.

[35.] Nestorius, whose disease is of an opposite kind, while pretending that he holds two distinct substances in Christ, brings in of a sudden two Persons, and with unheard of wickedness would have two sons of God, two Christs,--one, God, the other, man, one, begotten of his Father, the other, born of his mother. For which reason he maintains that Saint Mary ought to be called, not Theotocos (the mother of God), but Christotocos (the mother of Christ), seeing that she gave birth not to the Christ who is God, but to the Christ who is man. But if any one supposes that in his writings he speaks of one Christ, and preaches one Person of Christ, let him not lightly credit it. For either this is a crafty device, that by means of good he may the more easily persuade evil, according to that of the apostle, "That which is good was made death to me," [467] --either, I say, he craftily affects in some places in his writings to believe one Christ and one Person of Christ, or else he says that after the Virgin had brought forth, the two Persons were united into one Christ, though at the time of her conception or parturition, and for some short time afterwards, there were two Christs; so that forsooth, though Christ was born at first an ordinary man and nothing more, and not as yet associated in unity of Person with the Word of God, yet afterwards the Person of the Word assuming descended upon Him; and though now the Person assumed remains in the glory of God, yet once there would seem to have been no difference between Him and all other men.

[466] "Et hoc ipsum non plena fidei sanitate."--The Cambridge Ed., 1687, with Baluzius's notes appended, reads, "et hoc ipsum plena fidei sanctitate."

[467] Rom. vii. 13.

Chapter XIII.
The Catholic Doctrine of the Trinity and the Incarnation explained.

[36.] In these ways then do these rabid dogs, Nestorius, Apollinaris, and Photinus, bark against the Catholic faith: Photinus, by denying the Trinity; Apollinaris, by teaching that the nature of the Word is mutable, and refusing to acknowledge that there are two substances in Christ, denying moreover either that Christ had a soul at all, or, at all events, that he had a rational soul, and asserting that the Word of God supplied the place of the rational soul; Nestorius, by affirming that there were always or at any rate that once there were two Christs. But the Catholic Church, holding the right faith both concerning God and concerning our Saviour, is guilty of blasphemy neither in the mystery of the Trinity, nor in that of the Incarnation of Christ. For she worships both one Godhead in the plenitude of the Trinity, and the equality of the Trinity in one and the same majesty, and she confesses one Christ Jesus, not two; the same both God and man, the one as truly as the other. [468] One Person indeed she believes in Him, but two substances; two substances but one Person: Two substances, because the Word of God is not mutable, so as to be convertible into flesh; one Person, lest by acknowledging two sons she should seem to worship not a Trinity, but a Quaternity.

[37.] But it will be well to unfold this same doctrine more distinctly and explicitly again and again.

In God there is one substance, but three Persons; in Christ two substances, but one Person. In the Trinity, another and another Person, not another and another substance (distinct Persons, not distinct substances); [469] in the Saviour another and another substance, not another and another Person, (distinct substances, not distinct Persons). How in the Trinity another and another Person (distinct Persons) not another and another substance (distinct substances)? [470] Because there is one Person of the Father, another of the Son, another of the Holy Ghost; [471] but yet there is not another and another nature (distinct natures) but one and the same nature. How in the Saviour another and another substance, not another and another Person (two distinct substances, not two distinct Persons)? Because there is one substance of the Godhead, another of the manhood. But yet the Godhead and the manhood are not another and another Person (two distinct Persons), but one and the same Christ, one and the same Son of God, and one and the same Person of one and the same Christ and Son of God, in like manner as in man the flesh is one thing and the soul another, but one and the same man, both soul and flesh. In Peter and Paul the soul is one thing, the flesh another; yet there are not two Peters,--one soul, the other flesh, or two Pauls, one soul, the other flesh,--but one and the same Peter, and one and the same Paul, consisting each of two diverse natures, soul and body. Thus, then, in one and the same Christ there are two substances, one divine, the other human; one of (ex) God the Father, the other of (ex) the Virgin Mother; one co-eternal with and co-equal with the Father, the other temporal and inferior to the Father; one consubstantial with his Father, the other, consubstantial with his Mother, but one and the same Christ in both substances. There is not, therefore, one Christ God, the other man, not one uncreated, the other created; not one impassible, the other passible; not one equal to the Father, the other inferior to the Father; not one of his Father (ex), the other of his Mother (ex), but one and the same Christ, God and man, the same uncreated and created, the same unchangeable and incapable of suffering, the same acquainted by experience with both change and suffering, the same equal to the Father and inferior to the Father, the same begotten of the Father before time, ("before the world"), the same born of his mother in time ("in the world"), [472] perfect God, perfect Man. In God supreme divinity, in man perfect humanity. Perfect humanity, I say, forasmuch as it hath both soul and flesh; the flesh, very flesh; our flesh, his mother's flesh; the soul, intellectual, endowed with mind and reason. There is then in Christ the Word, the soul, the flesh; but the whole is one Christ, one Son of God, and one our Saviour and Redeemer: One, not by I know not what corruptible confusion of Godhead and manhood, but by a certain entire and singular unity of Person. For the conjunction hath not converted and changed the one nature into the other, (which is the characteristic error of the Arians), but rather hath in such wise compacted both into one, that while there always remains in Christ the singularity of one and the self-same Person, there abides eternally withal the characteristic property of each nature; whence it follows, that neither doth God (i.e., the divine nature) ever begin to be body, nor doth the body ever cease to be body. The which may be illustrated in human nature: for not only in the present life, but in the future also, each individual man will consist of soul and body; nor will his body ever be converted into soul, or his soul into body; but while each individual man will live for ever, the distinction between the two substances will continue in each individual man for ever. So likewise in Christ each substance will for ever retain its own characteristic property, yet without prejudice to the unity of Person.

[468] Unum Christum Jesum non duos, eundemque Deum pariter atque Hominem confitetur. Compare the Athanasian Creed, "Est ergo fides recta et credamus et confiteamur, quia Dominus Noster Jesus Christus. Dei Filius, Deus pariter et Homo est."

[469] In Trinitate alius atque alius, non aliud atque aliud. In Salvatore aliud atque aliud, non alius atque alius.

[470] Aliud atque aliud, non alius atque alius.

[471] Quia scilicet alia est Persona Patris, alia Filii, alia Spiritus Sancti sed tamen Patris et Filii et Spiritus Sancti

non alia et alia sed una cadunque natura. So the Athanasian Creed, "Alia est enim Persona Patris, alia Filii, alia Spiritus Sancti, sed Patris et Filii et Spiritus Sancti una est Divinitas, etc." The coincidence between the whole of this context and the Athanasian Creed is very observable, though the agreement is not always exact to the very letter.

[472] Idem ex Patre ante saecula genitus, Idem in saeculo ex matre generatus. Compare the Athanasian Creed, "Deus est ex substantia Patris ante saecula genitus; Homo ex substantia Matris in saeculo natus." See Appendix I.

Chapter XIV.
Jesus Christ Man in Truth, not in Semblance.

[38.] But when we use the word "Person," and say that God became man by means of a Person, there is reason to fear that our meaning may be taken to be, that God the Word assumed our nature merely in imitation, and performed the actions of man, being man not in reality, but only in semblance, just as in a theatre, one man within a brief space represents several persons, not one of whom himself is. For when one undertakes to sustain the part of another, he performs the offices, or does the acts, of the person whose part he sustains, but he is not himself that person. So, to take an illustration from secular life and one in high favour with the Manichees, when a tragedian represents a priest or a king, he is not really a priest or a king. For, as soon as the play is over, the person or character whom he represented ceases to be. God forbid that we should have anything to do with such nefarious and wicked mockery. Be it the infatuation of the Manichees, those preachers of hallucination, who say that the Son of God, God, was not a human person really and truly, but that He counterfeited the person of a man in feigned conversation and manner of life.

[39.] But the Catholic Faith teaches that the Word of God became man in such wise, that He took upon Him our nature, not feignedly and in semblance, but in reality and truth, and performed human actions, not as though

He were imitating the actions of another, but as performing His own, and as being in reality the person whose part He sustained. Just as we ourselves also, when we speak, reason, live, subsist, do not imitate men, but are men. Peter and John, for instance, were men, not by imitation, but by being men in reality. Paul did not counterfeit an apostle, or feign himself to be Paul, but was an apostle, was Paul. So, also, that which God the Word did, in His condescension, in assuming and having flesh, in speaking, acting, and suffering, through the instrumentality of flesh, yet without any marring of His own divine nature, came in one word to this:--He did not imitate or feign Himself to be perfect man, but He shewed Himself to be very man in reality and truth. Therefore, as the soul united to the flesh, but yet not changed into flesh, does not imitate man, but is man, and man not feignedly but substantially, so also God the Word, without any conversion of Himself, in uniting Himself to man, became man, not by confusion, not by imitation, but by actually being and subsisting. Away then, once and for all, with the notion of His Person as of an assumed fictitious character, where always what is is one thing, what is counterfeited another, where the man who acts never is the man whose part he acts. God forbid that we should believe God the Word to have taken upon Himself the person of a man in this illusory way. Rather let us acknowledge that while His own unchangeable substance remained, and while He took upon Himself the nature of perfect man, Himself actually was flesh, Himself actually was man, Himself actually was personally man; not feignedly, but in truth, not in imitation, but in substance; not, finally, so as to cease to be when the performance was over, but so as to be, and continue to be substantially and permanently. [473]

[473] The word "Person" is used in this and the preceding section in a way which might seem at variance with Catholic truth. Christ did not assume the Person of a man; but, being God, He united in his one divine Person, the Godhead and the Manhood. This Vincentius himself teaches most explicitly. But his object here is to show that our blessed Lord, while conversant among us as man, and being to all appearance man, did not personate man, but was man in deed and in truth. The misconception against which Vincentius seeks to guard arises from the ambiguity of the Latin Persona, an ambiguity which is not continued in our derived word Person. Persona signifies not only Person, in our sense of the word, but also an assumed character. Though however we have not this sense in Person, we have it in Personate.

Chapter XV.
The Union of the Divine with the Human Nature took place in the very Conception of the Virgin. The appellation "The Mother of God."

[40.] This unity of Person, then, in Christ was not effected after His birth of the Virgin, but was compacted and perfected in her very womb. For we must take most especial heed that we confess Christ not only one, but always one. For it were intolerable blasphemy, if while thou dost confess Him one now, thou shouldst maintain that once He was not one, but two; one forsooth since His baptism, but two at His birth. Which monstrous sacrilege we shall assuredly in no wise avoid unless we acknowledge the manhood united to the Godhead (but by unity of Person), not from the ascension, or the resurrection, or the baptism, but even in His mother, even in the womb, even in the Virgin's very conception. [474] In consequence of which unity of Person, both those attributes which are proper to God are ascribed to man, and those which are proper to the flesh to God, indifferently and promiscuously. [475] For hence it is written by divine guidance, on the one hand, that the Son of man came down from heaven; [476] and on the other, that the Lord of glory was crucified on earth. [477] Hence it is also that since the Lord's flesh was made, since the Lord's flesh was created, the very Word of God is said to have been made, the very omniscient Wisdom of God to have been created, just as prophetically His hands and His feet are described as having been pierced. [478] From this unity of Person it follows, by reason of a like mystery, that, since the flesh of the Word was born of an undefiled mother, God the Word Himself is most Catholicly believed, most impiously denied, to have been born of the Virgin; which being the case, God forbid that any one should seek to defraud Holy Mary of her prerogative of divine grace and her special glory. For by the singular gift of Him who is our Lord and God, and withal, her own son, she is to be confessed most truly and most blessedly-- The mother of God "Theotocos," but not in the sense in which it is imagined by a certain impious heresy which maintains, that she is to be called the Mother of God for no other reason than because she gave birth to that man who afterwards became God, just as we speak of a woman as the mother of a priest, or the mother of a bishop, meaning that she was such, not by giving birth to one already a priest or a bishop, but by giving birth to one who afterwards became a priest or a bishop. Not thus, I say, was the holy Mary "Theotocos," the mother of God, but rather, as was said before, because in her sacred womb was wrought that most sacred mystery whereby, on account of the singular and unique unity of Person, as the Word in flesh is flesh, so Man in God is God. [479]

[474] If the Son of God had taken to Himself a man now made and already perfected, it would of necessity follow that there are in Christ two persons, the one

assuming and the other assumed; whereas, the Son of God did not assume a man's person unto His own, but a man's nature to His own person, and therefore took semen, the seed of Abraham, the very first original element of our nature, before it was come to have any personal human subsistence. The flesh, and the conjunction of the flesh with God, began both in one instant. His making and taking to Himself our flesh was but one act, so that in Christ there is no personal subsistence but one, and that from everlasting. By taking only the nature of man He still continueth one person, and changeth but the manner of His subsisting, which was before in the mere glory of the Son of God and is now in the habit of our flesh.--Hooker, Eccl. Pol. v. 52, S: 3.

[475] "A kind of mutual commutation there is, whereby those concrete names, God and man, when we speak of Christ, do take interchangeably one another's room, so that for truth of speech, it skilleth not, whether we say that the Son of God hath created the world, and the Son of man by His death hath saved it, or else, that the Son of man did create, and the Son of God die to save the world. Howbeit, as oft as we attribute to God what the manhood of Christ claimeth, or to man what His Deity hath right unto, we understand by the name of God and the name of man neither the one nor the other nature, but the whole person of Christ, in whom both natures are."--Hooker, Eccl. Polity, v. 53, S: 4. This is technically

called "The Communication of Properties," Communicatio idiomatum.

[476] St. John iii. 13.

[477] 1 Cor. ii. 8.

[478] Ps. xxii. 16.

[479] Sicut Verbum in carne caro, ita Homo in Deo Deus est. Compare the Athanasian Creed, v. 33, in what is probably the true reading, "Unus autem, non conversione Divinitatis in carne, sed assumptione Humanitatis in Deo."

Chapter XVI.
Recapitulation of what was said of the Catholic Faith and of divers Heresies, Chapters xi-xv.

[41.] But now that we may refresh our remembrance of what has been briefly said concerning either the afore-mentioned heresies or the Catholic Faith, let us go over it again more briefly and concisely, that being repeated it may be more thoroughly understood, and being pressed home more firmly held.

Accursed then be Photinus, who does not receive the Trinity complete, but asserts that Christ is mere man.

Accursed be Apollinaris, who affirms that the Godhead of Christ is marred by conversion, and defrauds Him of the property of perfect humanity.

Accursed be Nestorius, who denies that God was born of the Virgin, affirms two Christs, and rejecting the belief of the Trinity, brings in a Quaternity.

But blessed be the Catholic Church, which worships one God in the completeness of the Trinity, and at the same time adores the equality of the Trinity in the unity of the Godhead, so that neither the singularity of substance confounds the propriety of the Persons, not the distinction of the Persons in the Trinity separates the unity of the Godhead.

Blessed, I say, be the Church, which believes that in Christ there are two true and perfect substances but one Person, so that neither doth the distinction of natures divide the unity of Person, nor the unity of Person confound the distinction of substances.

Blessed, I say, be the Church, which understands God to have become Man, not by conversion of nature, but by reason of a Person, but of a Person not feigned and transient, but substantial and permanent.

Blessed, I say, be the Church, which declares this unity of Person to be so real and effectual, that because of it, in a marvellous and ineffable mystery, she ascribes divine attributes to man, and human to God; because of it, on the one hand, she does not deny that Man, as God, came down from heaven, on the other, she believes that God, as Man, was created, suffered, and was crucified on earth; because of it, finally, she confesses Man the Son of God, and God the Son of the Virgin.

Blessed, then, and venerable, blessed and most sacred, and altogether worthy to be compared with those celestial praises of the Angelic Host, be the confession which ascribes glory to the one Lord God with a threefold ascription of holiness. For this reason moreover she insists emphatically upon the oneness of the Person of Christ, that she may not go beyond the mystery of the Trinity (that is by making in effect a Quaternity.)

Thus much by way of digression. On another occasion, please God, we will deal with the subject and unfold it more fully. [480] Now let us return to the matter in hand.

[480] Anrtelmi, who ascribed the Athanasian Creed to Vincentius, thought that document a fulfilment of the promise here made. Nova de Symbolo Athanasiano Disquisitio.--See Appendix I.

Chapter XVII.
The Error of Origen a great Trial to the Church.

[42.] We said above that in the Church of God the teacher's error is the people's trial, a trial by so much the greater in proportion to the greater learning of the erring teacher. This we showed first by the authority of Scripture, and then by instances from Church History, of persons who having at one time had the reputation of being sound in the faith, eventually either fell away to some sect already in existence, or else founded a heresy of their own. An important fact truly, useful to be learnt, and necessary to be remembered, and to be illustrated and enforced again and again, by example upon example, in order that all true Catholics may understand that it behoves them with the Church to receive Teachers, not with Teachers to desert the faith of the Church.

[43.] My belief is, that among many instances of this sort of trial which might be produced, there is not one to be compared with that of Origen, [481] in whom there were many things so excellent, so unique, so admirable, that antecedently any one would readily deem that implicit faith was to be placed all his assertions. For if the conversation and manner of life carry authority, great was his industry, great his modesty, his patience, his endurance; if his descent or his erudition, what more noble than his birth of a house rendered illustrious by martyrdom? Afterwards, when in the cause of Christ he had been deprived not only of his father, but also of all his property, he attained so high a standard in the midst of the straits of holy poverty, that he suffered several times, it is said, as a Confessor. Nor were these the only circumstances connected with him, all of which afterwards proved an occasion of trial. He had a genius so powerful, so profound, so acute, so elegant, that there was hardly any one whom he did not very far surpass. The splendour of his learning, and of his erudition generally, was such that there were few points of divine philosophy, hardly any of human which he did not thoroughly master. When Greek had yielded to his industry, he made himself a proficient in Hebrew. What shall I say of his eloquence, the style of which was so charming, so soft, so sweet, that honey rather than words seemed to flow from his mouth! What subjects were there, however difficult, which he did not render clear and perspicuous by the force of his reasoning? What undertakings, however hard to accomplish, which he did not make to appear most easy? But perhaps his assertions rested simply on ingeniously woven argumentation? On the contrary, no teacher ever used more proofs drawn from Scripture. Then I suppose he wrote little? No man more, so that, if I mistake not, his writings not only cannot all be read through, they cannot all be found; [482] for that nothing might be wanting to his opportunities of obtaining knowledge, he had the additional advantage of a life greatly prolonged. [483] But perhaps he was not particularly happy in his disciples? Who ever more so? From his school came forth doctors, priests, confessors, martyrs, without number. [484] Then who can express how much he was admired by all, how great his renown, how wide his influence? Who was there whose religion was at all above the common standard that did not hasten to him from the ends of the earth? What Christian did not reverence him almost as a prophet; what philosopher as a master? How great was the veneration with which he was regarded, not only by private persons, but also by the Court, is declared by the histories which relate how he was sent for by the mother of the Emperor Alexander, [485] moved by the heavenly wisdom with the love of which she, as he, was inflamed. To this also his letters bear witness, which, with the authority which he assumed as a Christian Teacher, he wrote to the Emperor Philip, [486] the first Roman prince that was a Christian. As to his incredible learning, if any one is unwilling to receive the testimony of Christians at our hands, let him at least accept that of heathens at the hands of philosophers. For that impious Porphyry says that when he was little more than a boy, incited by his fame, he went to Alexandria, and there saw him, then an old man, but a man evidently of so great attainments, that he had reached the summit of universal knowledge.

[44.] Time would fail me to recount, even in a very small measure, the excellencies of this man, all of which, nevertheless, not only contributed to the glory of religion, but also increased the magnitude of the trial. For who in the world would lightly desert a man of so great genius, so great learning, so great influence, and would not rather adopt that saying, That he would rather be wrong with Origen, than be right with others. [487]

What shall I say more? The result was that very many were led astray from the integrity of the faith, not by any human excellencies of this so great man, this so great doctor, this so great prophet, but, as the event showed, by the too perilous trial which he proved to be. Hence it came to pass, that this Origen, such and so great as he was, wantonly abusing the grace of God, rashly following the bent of his own genius, and placing overmuch confidence in himself, making light account of the ancient simplicity of the Christian religion, presuming that he knew more than all the world besides, despising the traditions of the Church and the determinations of the ancients, and interpreting certain passages of Scripture in a novel way, deserved for himself the warning given to the Church of God, as applicable in his case as in that of others, "If there arise a prophet in the midst of thee,"... "thou shalt not hearken to the words of that prophet,"..."because the Lord your God doth make trial of you, whether you love Him or not." [488] Truly, thus of a sudden to seduce the Church which was devoted to him, and hung upon him through admiration of his genius, his learning, his eloquence, his manner of life and influence, while she had no fear, no suspicion for herself,--thus, I say, to seduce the Church, slowly and little by little, from the old religion to a new profaneness, was not only a trial, but a great trial. [489]

[45.] But some one will say, Origen's books have been corrupted. I do not deny it; nay, I grant it readily. For that such is the case has been handed down both orally and in writing, not only by Catholics, but by heretics as well. But the point is, that though himself be not, yet books published under his name are, a great trial, which, abounding in many hurtful blasphemies, are both read and delighted in, not as being some one else's, but as being believed to be his, so that, although there was no error in Origen's original meaning, yet Origen's authority appears to be an effectual cause in leading people to embrace error.

[481] Origen was born of Christian parents, at Alexandria, about the year 186. His father, Leonidas, suffered martyrdom in the persecution under Severus, in 202; and the family estate having been confiscated, his mother, with six younger children, became dependent upon him for her support. At the age of eighteen he was appointed by the bishop Demetrius over the Catechetical School of Alexandria, the duties of which place he discharged with eminent ability and success. He remained a layman till the age of forty-three, when he was admitted to priest's orders at Caesarea, greatly to the displeasure of Demetrius, by whose hand, according to the Church's rule, the office ought to have been conferred, and he was in consequence banished from Alexandria. Returning to Caesarea, he taught there with great reputation, and had many eminent persons among his disciples. He suffered much in the Decian

persecution in 250, when he was thrown into prison and subjected to severe tortures. His works, as Vincentius says, were very numerous, including among them the Hexapla, a revised edition of the Hebrew Scriptures and of the Septuagint version, together with three other versions, the Hebrew being set forth in both Hebrew and Greek characters. His writings were corrupted in many instances, so that, as Vincentius says, opinions were often imputed to him which he would not have acknowledged. He died in his sixty-ninth year at Tyre, and was buried there.

[482] "Quis nostrum," says St. Jerome, "potest tanta legere quanta ille conscripsit."--Hieron. ad Pam. et Occan.

[483] He died, as was said in the preceding note, in his sixty-ninth year.

[484] Among these were Gregory Thaumaturgus, Bishop of NeoCaesarea in Pontus, and Firmilian, Bishop of Caesarea in Cappadocia.

[485] Mammea.

[486] These are St. Jerome's words, from whose book, De Viris illustribus c. 54, Vincentius's account of Origen is taken. The vexed question of Philip's claim to be ranked as a Christian is discussed by Tillemont.--Histoire des Empereurs, T. iii. pp. 494 sqq.

[487] Errare malo cum Platone quam cum istis vera sentire.--Cicero, Tuscul. Quaest. 1.

[488] Deuteronomy xiii. 1.

[489] "The great Origen died after his many labors in peace. His immediate pupils were saints and rulers in the Church. He has the praise of St. Athanasius, St. Basil, and St. Gregory Nazianzen, and furnishes materials to St. Ambrose and St. Hilary; yet, as time proceeded a definite heterodoxy was the growing result of his theology, and at length, three hundred years after his death, he was condemned, and, as has generally been considered, in an OEcumenical Council."--Newman on Development, p. 85, First Edition.

Chapter XVIII.
Tertullian a great Trial to the Church.

[46.] The case is the same with Tertullian. [490] For as Origen holds by far the first place among the Greeks, so does Tertullian among the Latins. For who more learned than he, who more versed in knowledge whether divine or human? With marvellous capacity of mind he comprehended all philosophy, and had a knowledge of all schools of philosophers, and of the founders and upholders of schools, and was acquainted with all their rules and observances, and with their various histories and studies. Was not his genius of such unrivalled strength and vehemence that there was scarcely any obstacle which he proposed to himself to overcome, that he did not penetrate by acuteness, or crush by weight? As to his style, who can sufficiently set forth its praise? It was knit together with so much cogency of argument that it compelled assent, even where it failed to persuade. Every word almost was a sentence; every sentence a victory. This know the Marcions, the Apelleses, the Praxeases, the Hermogeneses, the Jews, the Heathens, the Gnostics, and the rest, whose blasphemies he overthrew by the force of his many and ponderous volumes, as with so many thunderbolts. Yet this man also, notwithstanding all that I have mentioned, this Tertullian, I say, too little tenacious of Catholic doctrine, that is, of the universal and ancient faith, more eloquent by far than faithful, [491] changed his belief, and justified what the blessed Confessor, Hilary, writes of him, namely, that "by his subsequent error he detracted from the authority of his approved writings." [492] He also was a great trial in the Church. But of Tertullian I am unwilling to say more. This only I will add, that, contrary to the injunction of Moses, by asserting the novel furies of Montanus [493] which arose in the Church, and those mad dreams of new doctrine dreamed by mad women, to be true prophecies, he deservedly made both himself and his writings obnoxious to the words, "If there arise a prophet in the midst of thee,"..."thou shalt not hearken to the words of that prophet. "For why? "Because the Lord your God doth make trial of you, whether you love Him or not."

[490] Hardly anything is known of Tertullian, besides what may be gathered from his works, in addition to the following account given by St. Jerome (De Viris Illustribus), which I quote from Bishop Kaye's work on Tertullian and his writings: "Tertullian, a presbyter, the first Latin writer after Victor and Apollonius, was a native of the province of Africa and city of Carthage, the son of a proconsular centurion. He was a man of a sharp and vehement temper, flourished under Severus and Caracalla, and wrote numerous works which, as they are generally known, I think it unnecessary to particularize. I saw at Concordia, in Italy, an old man named Paulus who said that, when young, he had met at Rome with an aged amanuensis of the blessed Cyprian, who told him that Cyprian never passed a day without reading some

portion of Tertullian's works, and used frequently to say, Give me my master,' meaning Tertullian. After remaining a presbyter of the Church till he had attained the middle of life, Tertullian was by the cruel and contumelious treatment of the Roman clergy driven to embrace the opinions of Montanus, which he has mentioned in several of his works, under the title of The New Prophecy.' He is reported to have lived to a very advanced age." He was born about the middle of the second century, and flourished, according to the dates indicated above, between the years 190 and 216.

[491] Fidelior, Baluz, Felicior, others.

[492] In Mat. v.

[493] Montanus, with his two prophetesses, professed that he was intrusted with a new dispensation,--a dispensation in advance of the Gospel, as the Gospel was in advance of the Law. His system was a protest against the laxity which had grown up in the Church, as has repeatedly been the case after revivals of religious fervor, verifying Tertullian's apophthegm, "Christiani fiunt, non nascuntur" (men become Christians, they are not born such). Its characteristics were extreme asceticism, rigorous fasting, the exaltation of celibacy, the absolute prohibition of second marriage, the expectation of our Lord's second advent as near at hand, the disparagement of the clergy in comparison with its own Paraclete-inspired teachers. It had its rise in Phrygia, and from thence spread throughout Asia Minor, thence it found its

way to Southern Gaul, to Rome, to North Western
Africa, in which last for a time it had many followers.

Chapter XIX.
What we ought to learn from these Examples.

[47.] It behoves us, then, to give heed to these instances from Church History, so many and so great, and others of the same description, and to understand distinctly, in accordance with the rule laid down in Deuteronomy, that if at any time a Doctor in the Church have erred from the faith, Divine Providence permits it in order to make trial of us, whether or not we love God with all our heart and with all our mind.

Chapter XX.
The Notes of a true Catholic.

[48.] This being the case, he is the true and genuine
Catholic who loves the truth of God, who loves the
Church, who loves the Body of Christ, who esteems
divine religion and the Catholic Faith above every thing,
above the authority, above the regard, above the genius,
above the eloquence, above the philosophy, of every
man whatsoever; who sets light by all of these, and
continuing steadfast and established in the faith, resolves
that he will believe that, and that only, which he is sure
the Catholic Church has held universally and from
ancient time; but that whatsoever new and unheard-of
doctrine he shall find to have been furtively introduced
by some one or another, besides that of all, or contrary
to that of all the saints, this, he will understand, does not
pertain to religion, but is permitted as a trial, being
instructed especially by the words of the blessed Apostle
Paul, who writes thus in his first Epistle to the
Corinthians, "There must needs be heresies, that they
who are approved may be made manifest among you:"
[494] as though he should say, This is the reason why the
authors of Heresies are not forthwith rooted up by God,
namely, that they who are approved may be made
manifest; that is, that it may be apparent of each
individual, how tenacious and faithful and steadfast he is
in his love of the Catholic faith.

[49.] And in truth, as each novelty springs up incontinently is discerned the difference between the weight of the wheat and the lightness of the chaff. Then that which had no weight to keep it on the floor is without difficulty blown away. For some at once fly off entirely; others having been only shaken out, afraid of perishing, wounded, half alive, half dead, are ashamed to return. They have, in fact swallowed a quantity of poison--not enough to kill, yet more than can be got rid of; it neither causes death, nor suffers to live. O wretched condition! With what surging tempestuous cares are they tossed about! One while, the error being set in motion, they are hurried whithersoever the wind drives them; another, returning upon themselves like refluent waves, they are dashed back: one while, with rash presumption, they give their approval to what seems uncertain; another, with irrational fear, they are frightened out of their wits at what is certain, in doubt whither to go, whither to return, what to seek, what to shun, what to keep, what to throw away.

[50.] This affliction, indeed, of a hesitating and miserably vacillating mind is, if they are wise, a medicine intended for them by God's compassion. For therefore it is that outside the most secure harbour of the Catholic Faith, they are tossed about, beaten, and almost killed, by divers tempestuous cogitations, in order that they may take in the sails of self-conceit, which, they had with ill advice unfurled to the blasts of novelty, and may betake themselves again to, and remain stationary within, the most secure harbour of their placid and good mother, and may begin by vomiting up those bitter and turbid floods of error which they had swallowed, that thenceforward they may be able to drink the streams of fresh and living water. Let them unlearn well what they had learnt not well, and let them receive so much of the entire doctrine of the Church as they can understand: what they cannot understand let them believe.

[494] 1 Cor. ii. 9.

Chapter XXI.
Exposition of St. Paul's Words.--1 Tim. vi. 20.

[51.] Such being the case, when I think over these things, and revolve them in my mind again and again, I cannot sufficiently wonder at the madness of certain men, at the impiety of their blinded understanding, at their lust of error, such that, not content with the rule of faith delivered once for all, and received from the times of old, they are every day seeking one novelty after another, and are constantly longing to add, change, take away, in religion, as though the doctrine, "Let what has once for all been revealed suffice," were not a heavenly but an earthly rule,--a rule which could not be complied with except by continual emendation, nay, rather by continual fault-finding; whereas the divine Oracles cry aloud, "Remove not the landmarks, which thy fathers have set," [495] and "Go not to law with a Judge," [496] and "Whoso breaketh through a fence a serpent shall bite him," [497] and that saying of the Apostle wherewith, as with a spiritual sword, all the wicked novelties of all heresies often have been, and will always have to be, decapitated, "O Timothy, keep the deposit, shunning profane novelties of words and oppositions of the knowledge falsely so called, which some professing have erred concerning the faith." [498]

[52.] After words such as these, is there any one of so hardened a front, such anvil-like impudence, such adamantine pertinacity, as not to succumb to so huge a mass, not to be crushed by so ponderous a weight, not to be shaken in pieces by such heavy blows, not to be annihilated by such dreadful thunderbolts of divine eloquence? "Shun profane novelties," he says. He does not say shun "antiquity." But he plainly points to what ought to follow by the rule of contrary. For if novelty is to be shunned, antiquity is to be held fast; if novelty is profane, antiquity is sacred. He adds, "And oppositions of science falsely so called." "Falsely called" indeed, as applied to the doctrines of heretics, where ignorance is disguised under the name of knowledge, fog of sunshine, darkness of light. "Which some professing have erred concerning the faith." Professing what? What but some (I know not what) new and unheard-of doctrine. For thou mayest hear some of these same doctors say, "Come, O silly wretches, who go by the name of Catholics, come and learn the true faith, which no one but ourselves is acquainted with, which same has lain hid these many ages, but has recently been revealed and made manifest. But learn it by stealth and in secret, for you will be delighted with it. Moreover, when you have learnt it, teach it furtively, that the world may not hear, that the Church may not know. For there are but few to whom it is granted to receive the secret of so great a mystery." Are not these the words of that harlot who, in the proverbs of Solomon, calls to the passengers who go right on their ways, "Whoso is simple let him turn in hither." And as for them that are void of understanding, she exhorts them saying: "Drink stolen waters, for they are sweet, and eat bread in secret for it is pleasant." What next? "But he knoweth not that the sons of earth perish in her house." [499] Who are those "sons of earth"? Let the apostle explain: "Those who have erred concerning the faith."

[495] Prov. xxii. 28.

[496] Ecclus. viii. 14.

[497] Eccles. x. 8.

[498] 1 Tim. vi. 20.

[499] Prov. ix. 16-18.

Chapter XXII.
A more particular Exposition of 1 Tim. vi. 20.

[53.] But it is worth while to expound the whole of that passage of the apostle more fully, "O Timothy, keep the deposit, avoiding profane novelties of words."

"O!" The exclamation implies fore-knowledge as well as charity. For he mourned in anticipation over the errors which he foresaw. Who is the Timothy of to-day, but either generally the Universal Church, or in particular, the whole body of The Prelacy, whom it behoves either themselves to possess or to communicate to others a complete knowledge of religion? What is "Keep the deposit"? "Keep it," because of thieves, because of adversaries, lest, while men sleep, they sow tares over that good wheat which the Son of Man had sown in his field. "Keep the deposit." What is "The deposit"? That which has been intrusted to thee, not that which thou hast thyself devised: a matter not of wit, but of learning; not of private adoption, but of public tradition; a matter brought to thee, not put forth by thee, wherein thou art bound to be not an author but a keeper, not a teacher but a disciple, not a leader but a follower. "Keep the deposit." Preserve the talent of Catholic Faith inviolate, unadulterate. That which has been intrusted to thee, let it continue in thy possession, let it be handed on by thee. Thou hast received gold; give gold in turn. Do not substitute one thing for another. Do not for gold impudently substitute lead or brass. Give real gold, not counterfeit.

O Timothy! O Priest! O Expositor! O Doctor! if the divine gift hath qualified thee by wit, by skill, by learning, be thou a Bazaleel of the spiritual tabernacle, [500] engrave the precious gems of divine doctrine, fit them in accurately, adorn them skilfully, add splendor, grace, beauty. Let that which formerly was believed, though imperfectly apprehended, as expounded by thee be clearly understood. Let posterity welcome, understood through thy exposition, what antiquity venerated without understanding. Yet teach still the same truths which thou hast learnt, so that though thou speakest after a new fashion, what thou speakest may not be new.

[500] Exod. xxxi. 1, etc.

Chapter XXIII.
On Development in Religious Knowledge.

[54.] But some one will say, perhaps, Shall there, then, be no progress in Christ's Church? Certainly; all possible progress. For what being is there, so envious of men, so full of hatred to God, who would seek to forbid it? Yet on condition that it be real progress, not alteration of the faith. For progress requires that the subject be enlarged in itself, alteration, that it be transformed into something else. The intelligence, then, the knowledge, the wisdom, as well of individuals as of all, as well of one man as of the whole Church, ought, in the course of ages and centuries, to increase and make much and vigorous progress; but yet only in its own kind; that is to say, in the same doctrine, in the same sense, and in the same meaning.

[55.] The growth of religion in the soul must be analogous to the growth of the body, which, though in process of years it is developed and attains its full size, yet remains still the same. There is a wide difference between the flower of youth and the maturity of age; yet they who were once young are still the same now that they have become old, insomuch that though the stature and outward form of the individual are changed, yet his nature is one and the same, his person is one and the same. An infant's limbs are small, a young man's large, yet the infant and the young man are the same. Men when full grown have the same number of joints that they had when children; and if there be any to which maturer age has given birth these were already present in embryo, so that nothing new is produced in them when old which was not already latent in them when children. This, then, is undoubtedly the true and legitimate rule of progress, this the established and most beautiful order of growth, that mature age ever develops in the man those parts and forms which the wisdom of the Creator had already framed beforehand in the infant. Whereas, if the human form were changed into some shape belonging to another kind, or at any rate, if the number of its limbs were increased or diminished, the result would be that the whole body would become either a wreck or a monster, or, at the least, would be impaired and enfeebled.

[56.] In like manner, it behoves Christian doctrine to follow the same laws of progress, so as to be consolidated by years, enlarged by time, refined by age, and yet, withal, to continue uncorrupt and unadulterate, complete and perfect in all the measurement of its parts, and, so to speak, in all its proper members and senses, admitting no change, no waste of its distinctive property, no variation in its limits.

[57.] For example: Our forefathers in the old time sowed wheat in the Church's field. It would be most unmeet and iniquitous if we, their descendants, instead of the genuine truth of corn, should reap the counterfeit error of tares. This rather should be the result,--there should be no discrepancy between the first and the last. From doctrine which was sown as wheat, we should reap, in the increase, doctrine of the same kind--wheat also; so that when in process of time any of the original seed is developed, and now flourishes under cultivation, no change may ensue in the character of the plant. There may supervene shape, form, variation in outward appearance, but the nature of each kind must remain the same. God forbid that those rose-beds of Catholic interpretation should be converted into thorns and thistles. God forbid that in that spiritual paradise from plants of cinnamon and balsam, darnel and wolfsbane should of a sudden shoot forth.

Therefore, whatever has been sown by the fidelity of the Fathers in this husbandry of God's Church, the same ought to be cultivated and taken care of by the industry of their children, the same ought to flourish and ripen, the same ought to advance and go forward to perfection. For it is right that those ancient doctrines of heavenly philosophy should, as time goes on, be cared for, smoothed, polished; but not that they should be changed, not that they should be maimed, not that they should be mutilated. They may receive proof, illustration, definiteness; but they must retain withal their completeness, their integrity, their characteristic properties.

[58.] For if once this license of impious fraud be admitted, I dread to say in how great danger religion will be of being utterly destroyed and annihilated. For if any one part of Catholic truth be given up, another, and another, and another will thenceforward be given up as a matter of course, and the several individual portions having been rejected, what will follow in the end but the rejection of the whole? On the other hand, if what is new begins to be mingled with what is old, foreign with domestic, profane with sacred, the custom will of necessity creep on universally, till at last the Church will have nothing left untampered with, nothing unadulterated, nothing sound, nothing pure; but where formerly there was a sanctuary of chaste and undefiled truth, thenceforward there will be a brothel of impious and base errors. May God's mercy avert this wickedness from the minds of his servants; be it rather the frenzy of the ungodly.

[59.] But the Church of Christ, the careful and watchful guardian of the doctrines deposited in her charge, never changes anything in them, never diminishes, never adds, does not cut off what is necessary, does not add what is superfluous, does not lose her own, does not appropriate what is another's, but while dealing faithfully and judiciously with ancient doctrine, keeps this one object carefully in view,--if there be anything which antiquity has left shapeless and rudimentary, to fashion and polish it, if anything already reduced to shape and developed, to consolidate and strengthen it, if any already ratified and defined, to keep and guard it. Finally, what other object have Councils ever aimed at in their decrees, than to provide that what was before believed in simplicity should in future be believed intelligently, that what was before preached coldly should in future be preached earnestly, that what was before practised negligently should thenceforward be practised with double solicitude? This, I say, is what the Catholic Church, roused by the novelties of heretics, has accomplished by the decrees of her Councils,--this, and nothing else,--she has thenceforward consigned to posterity in writing what she had received from those of olden times only by tradition, comprising a great amount of matter in a few words, and often, for the better understanding, designating an old article of the faith by the characteristic of a new name. [501]

[501] For instance, the proper Deity of our Blessed Lord by the word "Homousios," consubstantial, of one substance, essence, nature.

Chapter XXIV.
Continuation of the Exposition of 1 Tim. vi. 20.

[60.] But let us return to the apostle. "O Timothy," he says, "Guard the deposit, shunning profane novelties of words." "Shun them as you would a viper, as you would a scorpion, as you would a basilisk, lest they smite you not only with their touch, but even with their eyes and breath." What is "to shun"? Not even to eat [502] with a person of this sort. What is "shun"? "If anyone," says St. John, "come to you and bring not this doctrine." What doctrine? What but the Catholic and universal doctrine, which has continued one and the same through the several successions of ages by the uncorrupt tradition of the truth and so will continue for ever--"Receive him not into your house, neither bid him Godspeed, for he that biddeth him Godspeed communicates with him in his evil deeds." [503]

[61.] "Profane novelties of words." What words are these? Such as have nothing sacred, nothing religious, words utterly remote from the inmost sanctuary of the Church which is the temple of God. "Profane novelties of words, that is, of doctrines, subjects, opinions, such as are contrary to antiquity and the faith of the olden time. Which if they be received, it follows necessarily that the faith of the blessed fathers is violated either in whole, or at all events in great part; it follows necessarily that all the faithful of all ages, all the saints, the chaste, the continent, the virgins, all the clergy, Deacons and Priests, so many thousands of Confessors, so vast an army of martyrs, such multitudes of cities and of peoples, so many islands, provinces, kings, tribes, kingdoms, nations, in a word, almost the whole earth, incorporated in Christ the Head, through the Catholic faith, have been ignorant for so long a tract of time, have been mistaken, have blasphemed, have not known what to believe, what to confess.

[62.] "Shun profane novelties of words," which to receive and follow was never the part of Catholics; of heretics always was. In sooth, what heresy ever burst forth save under a definite name, at a definite place, at a definite time? Who ever originated a heresy that did not first dissever himself from the consentient agreement of the universality and antiquity of the Catholic Church? That this is so is demonstrated in the clearest way by examples. For who ever before that profane Pelagius [504] attributed so much antecedent strength to Free-will, as to deny the necessity of God's grace to aid it towards good in every single act? Who ever before his monstrous disciple Coelestius denied that the whole human race is involved in the guilt of Adam's sin? Who ever before sacrilegious Arius dared to rend asunder the unity of the Trinity? Who before impious Sabellius was so audacious as to confound the Trinity of the Unity? Who before cruellest Novatian represented God as cruel in that He had rather the wicked should die than that he should be converted and live? Who before Simon

Magus, who was smitten by the apostle's rebuke, and from whom that ancient sink of every thing vile has flowed by a secret continuous succession even to Priscillian of our own time,--who, I say, before this Simon Magus, dared to say that God, the Creator, is the author of evil, that is, of our wickednesses, impieties, flagitiousnesses, inasmuch as he asserts that He created with His own hands a human nature of such a description, that of its own motion, and by the impulse of its necessity-constrained will, it can do nothing else, can will nothing else, but sin, seeing that tossed to and fro, and set on fire by the furies of all sorts of vices, it is hurried away by unquenchable lust into the utmost extremes of baseness?

[63.] There are innumerable instances of this kind, which for brevity's sake, pass over; by all of which, however, it is manifestly and clearly shown, that it is an established law, in the case of almost all heresies, that they evermore delight in profane novelties, scorn the decisions of antiquity, and, through oppositions of science falsely so called, make shipwreck of the faith. On the other hand, it is the sure characteristic of Catholics to keep that which has been committed to their trust by the holy Fathers, to condemn profane novelties, and, in the apostle's words, once and again repeated, to anathematize every one who preaches any other doctrine than that which has been received. [505]

[502] 1 Cor. v. 11.

[503] 2 John 10.

[504] Pelagius, a monk, a Briton by birth, resident in Rome, where by the strictness of his life he had acquired a high reputation for sanctity, was led, partly perhaps by opposition to St. Augustine's teaching on the subject of election and predestination, partly by indignation at the laxity of professing Christians, who pleaded, in excuse for their low standard, the weakness of human nature, to insist upon man's natural power, and to deny his need of divine grace. Pelagius was joined by another monk, Coelestius, a younger man, with whom about the year 410, the year in which Rome was taken by the Goths, he began to teach openly and in public what before he had held and taught in private. After the sack of Rome, the two friends passed over into Africa, and from thence Pelagius proceeded to Palestine, where he was in two separate synods acquitted of the charge of heresy which had been brought against him by Orosius, a Spanish monk, whom Augustine had sent for that purpose. But in 416, two African synods condemned his doctrine, and Zosimus bishop of Rome, whom he had appealed to, though he had set aside their decision, was eventually obliged to yield to the firmness with which they held their ground, and not only to condemn Pelagius, but to take stringent measures against his adherents. "In 418, another African synod of two hundred and fourteen bishops passed nine canons, which were afterwards generally accepted throughout the Church, and came to be regarded as the most important bulwark against

Pelagianism." The heresy was formally condemned, in 431, by the General Council of Ephesus. Canons 2 and 4. The Pelagians denied the corruption of man's nature, and the necessity of divine grace. They held that infants new-born are in the same state in which Adam was before his fall; that Adam's sin injured no one but himself, and affected his posterity no other wise than by the evil example which it afforded; they held also that men may live without sin if they will and that some have so lived. Those who were afterwards called semi-Pelagians (they belonged chiefly to the churches of Southern Gaul) were orthodox except in one particular: In their anxiety to justify, as they thought, God's dealings with man, they held that the first step in the way of salvation must be from ourselves: we must ask that we may receive, seek that we may find, knock that it may be opened to us; thenceforward in every stage of the road, our strenuous efforts must be aided by divine grace. They did not understand, or did not grant, that to that same grace must be referred even the disposition to ask, to seek, to knock. See Prosper's letter to Augustine, August. Opera, Tom. x. The semi-Pelagian doctrine was condemned in the second Council of Orange (a.d. 529), the third and fifth canons of which are directed against it.

[505] Gal. ii. 9.

Chapter XXV.
Heretics appeal to Scripture that they may more easily succeed in deceiving.

[64.] Here, possibly, some one may ask, Do heretics also appeal to Scripture? They do indeed, and with a vengeance; for you may see them scamper through every single book of Holy Scripture,--through the books of Moses, the books of Kings, the Psalms, the Epistles, the Gospels, the Prophets. Whether among their own people, or among strangers, in private or in public, in speaking or in writing, at convivial meetings, or in the streets, hardly ever do they bring forward anything of their own which they do not endeavour to shelter under words of Scripture. Read the works of Paul of Samosata, of Priscillian, of Eunomius, of Jovinian, and the rest of those pests, and you will see an infinite heap of instances, hardly a single page, which does not bristle with plausible quotations from the New Testament or the Old.

[65.] But the more secretly they conceal themselves under shelter of the Divine Law, so much the more are they to be feared and guarded against. For they know that the evil stench of their doctrine will hardly find acceptance with any one if it be exhaled pure and simple. They sprinkle it over, therefore, with the perfume of heavenly language, in order that one who would be ready to despise human error, may hesitate to condemn divine words. They do, in fact, what nurses do when they would prepare some bitter draught for children; they smear the edge of the cup all round with honey, that the unsuspecting child, having first tasted the sweet, may have no fear of the bitter. So too do these act, who disguise poisonous herbs and noxious juices under the names of medicines, so that no one almost, when he reads the label, suspects the poison.

[66.] It was for this reason that the Saviour cried, "Beware of false prophets who come to you in sheep's clothing, but inwardly they are ravening wolves." [506] What is meant by "sheep's clothing"? What but the words which prophets and apostles with the guilelessness of sheep wove beforehand as fleeces, for that immaculate Lamb which taketh away the sin of the world? What are the ravening wolves? What but the savage and rabid glosses of heretics, who continually infest the Church's folds, and tear in pieces the flock of Christ wherever they are able? But that they may with more successful guile steal upon the unsuspecting sheep, retaining the ferocity of the wolf, they put off his appearance, and wrap themselves, so to say, in the language of the Divine Law, as in a fleece, so that one, having felt the softness of wool, may have no dread of the wolf's fangs. But what saith the Saviour? "By their fruits ye shall know them;" that is, when they have begun not only to quote those divine words, but also to expound them, not as yet only to make a boast of them as on their side, but also to interpret them, then will that bitterness, that acerbity, that rage, be understood; then will the ill-savour of that novel poison be perceived, then will those profane novelties be disclosed, then may you see first the hedge broken through, then the landmarks of the Fathers removed, then the Catholic faith assailed, then the doctrine of the Church torn in pieces.

[67.] Such were they whom the Apostle Paul rebukes in his Second Epistle to the Corinthians, when he says, "For of this sort are false apostles, deceitful workers, transforming themselves into apostles of Christ." [507] The apostles brought forward instances from Holy Scripture; these men did the same. The apostles cited the authority of the Psalms; these men did so likewise. The apostles brought forward passages from the prophets; these men still did the same. But when they began to interpret in different senses the passages which both had agreed in appealing to, then were discerned the guileless from the crafty, the genuine from the counterfeit, the straight from the crooked, then, in one word, the true apostles from the false apostles. "And no wonder," he says, "for Satan himself transforms himself into an angel of light. It is no marvel then if his servants are transformed as the servants of righteousness." Therefore, according to the authority of the Apostle Paul, as often as either false apostles or false teachers cite passages from the Divine Law, by means of which, misinterpreted, they seek to prop up their own errors, there is no doubt that they are following the cunning devices of their father, which assuredly he would never have devised, but that he knew that where he could fraudulently and by stealth introduce error, there is no easier way of effecting his impious purpose than by pretending the authority of Holy Scripture.

[506] Matt. vii. 15.

[507] 2 Cor. xi. 12.

Chapter XXVI.
Heretics, in quoting Scripture, follow the example of the Devil.

[68.] But some one will say, What proof have we that the Devil is wont to appeal to Holy Scripture? Let him read the Gospels wherein it is written, "Then the Devil took Him (the Lord the Saviour) and set Him upon a pinnacle of the Temple, and said unto Him: If thou be the Son of God, cast thyself down, for it is written, He shall give His angels charge concerning thee, that they may keep thee in all thy ways: In their hands they shall bear thee up, lest perchance thou dash thy foot against a stone." [508] What sort of treatment must men, insignificant wretches that they are, look for at the hands of him who assailed even the Lord of Glory with quotations from Scripture? "If thou be the Son of God," saith he, "cast thyself down." Wherefore? "For," saith he, "it is written." It behoves us to pay special attention to this passage and bear it in mind, that, warned by so important an instance of Evangelical authority, we may be assured beyond doubt, when we find people alleging passages from the Apostles or Prophets against the Catholic Faith, that the Devil speaks through their mouths. For as then the Head spoke to the Head, so now also the members speak to the members, the members of the Devil to the members of Christ, misbelievers to believers, sacrilegious to religious, in one word, Heretics to Catholics.

[69.] But what do they say? "If thou be the Son of God, cast thyself down;" that is, If thou wouldst be a son of God, and wouldst receive the inheritance of the Kingdom of Heaven, cast thyself down; that is, cast thyself down from the doctrine and tradition of that sublime Church, which is imagined to be nothing less than the very temple of God. And if one should ask one of the heretics who gives this advice, How do you prove? What ground have you, for saying, that I ought to cast away the universal and ancient faith of the Catholic Church? he has the answer ready, "For it is written;" and forthwith he produces a thousand testimonies, a thousand examples, a thousand authorities from the Law, from the Psalms, from the apostles, from the Prophets, by means of which, interpreted on a new and wrong principle, the unhappy soul may be precipitated from the height of Catholic truth to the lowest abyss of heresy. Then, with the accompanying promises, the heretics are wont marvellously to beguile the incautious. For they dare to teach and promise, that in their church, that is, in the conventicle of their communion, there is a certain great and special and altogether personal grace of God, so that whosoever pertain to their number, without any labour, without any effort, without any industry, even though they neither ask, nor seek, nor knock, have such a dispensation from God, that, borne up by angel hands, that is, preserved by the protection of angels, it is impossible they should ever dash their feet against a stone, that is, that they should ever be offended. [509]

[508] Matt. iv. 5, etc.

[509] See Appendix II.

Chapter XXVII.
What Rule is to be observed in the Interpretation of Scripture.

[70.] But it will be said, If the words, the sentiments, the promises of Scripture, are appealed to by the Devil and his disciples, of whom some are false apostles, some false prophets and false teachers, and all without exception heretics, what are Catholics and the sons of Mother Church to do? How are they to distinguish truth from falsehood in the sacred Scriptures? They must be very careful to pursue that course which, in the beginning of this Commonitory, we said that holy and learned men had commended to us, that is to say, they must interpret the sacred Canon according to the traditions of the Universal Church and in keeping with the rules of Catholic doctrine, in which Catholic and Universal Church, moreover, they must follow universality, antiquity, consent. And if at any time a part opposes itself to the whole, novelty to antiquity, the dissent of one or a few who are in error to the consent of all or at all events of the great majority of Catholics, then they must prefer the soundness of the whole to the corruption of a part; in which same whole they must prefer the religion of antiquity to the profaneness of novelty; and in antiquity itself in like manner, to the temerity of one or of a very few they must prefer, first of all, the general decrees, if such there be, of a Universal Council, or if there be no such, then, what is next best, they must follow the consentient belief of many and great masters. Which rule having been faithfully, soberly, and scrupulously observed, we shall with little difficulty detect the noxious errors of heretics as they arise.

Chapter XXVIII.

In what Way, on collating the consentient opinions of the Ancient Masters, the Novelties of Heretics may be detected and condemned.

[71.] And here I perceive that, as a necessary sequel to the foregoing, I ought to show by examples in what way, by collating the consentient opinions of the ancient masters, the profane novelties of heretics may be detected and condemned. Yet in the investigation of this ancient consent of the holy Fathers we are to bestow our pains not on every minor question of the Divine Law, but only, at all events especially, where the Rule of Faith is concerned. Nor is this way of dealing with heresy to be resorted to always, or in every instance, but only in the case of those heresies which are new and recent, and that on their first arising, before they have had time to deprave the Rules of the Ancient Faith, and before they endeavour, while the poison spreads and diffuses itself, to corrupt the writings of the ancients. But heresies already widely diffused and of old standing are by no means to be thus dealt with, seeing that through lapse of time they have long had opportunity of corrupting the truth. And therefore, as to the more ancient schisms or heresies, we ought either to confute them, if need be, by the sole authority of the Scriptures, or at any rate, to shun them as having been already of old convicted and condemned by universal councils of the Catholic Priesthood.

[72.] Therefore, as soon as the corruption of each mischievous error begins to break forth, and to defend itself by filching certain passages of Scripture, and expounding them fraudulently and deceitfully, forthwith, the opinions of the ancients in the interpretation of the Canon are to be collected, whereby the novelty, and consequently the profaneness, whatever it may be, that arises, may both without any doubt be exposed, and without any tergiversation be condemned. But the opinions of those Fathers only are to be used for comparison, who living and teaching, holily, wisely, and with constancy, in the Catholic faith and communion, were counted worthy either to die in the faith of Christ, or to suffer death happily for Christ. Whom yet we are to believe on this condition, that that only is to be accounted indubitable, certain, established, which either all, or the more part, have supported and confirmed manifestly, frequently, persistently, in one and the same sense, forming, as it were, a consentient council of doctors, all receiving, holding, handing on the same doctrine. But whatsoever a teacher holds, other than all, or contrary to all, be he holy and learned, be he a bishop, be he a Confessor, be he a martyr, let that be regarded as a private fancy of his own, and be separated from the authority of common, public, general persuasion, lest, after the sacrilegious custom of heretics and schismatics, rejecting the ancient truth of the universal Creed, we follow, at the utmost peril of our eternal salvation, the newly devised error of one man.

[73.] Lest any one perchance should rashly think the holy and Catholic consent of these blessed fathers to be despised, the Apostle says, in the First Epistle to the Corinthians, "God hath placed some in the Church, first Apostles," [510] of whom himself was one; "secondly Prophets," such as Agabus, of whom we read in the Acts of the Apostles; [511] "then doctors," who are now called Homilists, Expositors, [512] whom the same apostle sometimes calls also "Prophets," because by them the mysteries of the Prophets are opened to the people. Whosoever, therefore, shall despise these, who had their appointment of God in His Church in their several times and places, when they are unanimous in Christ, in the interpretation of some one point of Catholic doctrine, despises not man, but God, from whose unity in the truth, lest any one should vary, the same Apostle earnestly protests, "I beseech you, brethren, that ye all speak the same thing, and that there be no divisions among you, but that ye be perfectly joined together in the same mind and in the same judgment." [513] But if any one dissent from their unanimous decision, let him listen to the words of the same apostle, "God is not the God of dissension but of peace;" [514] that is, not of him who departs from the unity of consent, but of those who remain steadfast in the peace of consent: "as," he continues, "I teach in all Churches of the saints," that is, of Catholics, which churches are therefore churches of the saints, because they continue steadfast in the communion of the faith.

[74.] And lest any one, disregarding every one else, should arrogantly claim to be listened to himself alone, himself alone to be believed, the Apostle goes on to say, "Did the word of God proceed from you, or did it come to you only?" And, lest this should be thought lightly spoken, he continues, "If any man seem to be a prophet or a spiritual person, let him acknowledge that the things which I write unto you are the Lord's commands." As to which, unless a man be a prophet or a spiritual person, that is, a master in spiritual matters, let him be as observant as possible of impartiality and unity, so as neither to prefer his own opinions to those of every one besides, nor to recede from the belief of the whole body. Which injunction, whoso ignores, shall be himself ignored; [515] that is, he who either does not learn what he does not know, or treats with contempt what he knows, shall be ignored, that is, shall be deemed unworthy to be ranked of God with those who are united to each other by faith, and equalled with each other by humility, than which I cannot imagine a more terrible evil. This it is however which, according to the Apostle's threatening, we see to have befallen Julian the Pelagian, [516] who either neglected to associate himself with the belief of his fellow Christians, or presumed to dissociate himself from it.

[75.] But it is now time to bring forward the exemplification which we promised, where and how the sentences of the holy Fathers have been collected together, so that in accordance with them, by the decree and authority of a council, the rule of the Church's faith may be settled. Which that it may be done the more conveniently, let this present Commonitory end here, so that the remainder which is to follow may be begun from a fresh beginning.

[The Second Book of the Commonitory is lost. Nothing of it remains but the conclusion: in other words, the recapitulation which follows.]

[510] 1 Cor. xii. 27, 28.

[511] Acts xi. 28.

[512] "Tractatores." St. Augustine's Expository Lectures on St. John's Gospel are entitled "Tractatus."

[513] 1 Cor. i. 10.

[514] 1 Cor. xiv. 33.

[515] 1 Cor. xiv. 33.

[516] Julian, bishop of Eclanum, a small town in Apulia or Campania, was one of nineteen bishops, who, having espoused the cause of Pelagius, and having refused to subscribe a circular letter issued by Zosimus, now adopting the decisions of the African Council (see above note p. 147) were deposed and banished. St. Augustine at his death left a work against Julian unfinished, "Opus imperfectum contra Julianum," in which he had been

engaged till the sickness of which he died put an end to his labours.

Chapter XXIX.
Recapitulation.

[76.] This being the case, it is now time that we should recapitulate, at the close of this second Commonitory, what was said in that and in the preceding.

We said above, that it has always been the custom of Catholics, and still is, to prove the true faith in these two ways; first by the authority of the Divine Canon, and next by the tradition of the Catholic Church. Not that the Canon alone does not of itself suffice for every question, but seeing that the more part, interpreting the divine words according to their own persuasion, take up various erroneous opinions, it is therefore necessary that the interpretation of divine Scripture should be ruled according to the one standard of the Church's belief, especially in those articles on which the foundations of all Catholic doctrine rest.

[77.] We said likewise, that in the Church itself regard must be had to the consentient voice of universality equally with that of antiquity, lest we either be torn from the integrity of unity and carried away to schism, or be precipitated from the religion of antiquity into heretical novelties. We said, further, that in this same ecclesiastical antiquity two points are very carefully and earnestly to be held in view by those who would keep clear of heresy: first, they should ascertain whether any decision has been given in ancient times as to the matter in question by the whole priesthood of the Catholic Church, with the authority of a General Council: and, secondly, if some new question should arise on which no such decision has been given, they should then have recourse to the opinions of the holy Fathers, of those at least, who, each in his own time and place, remaining in the unity of communion and of the faith, were accepted as approved masters; and whatsoever these may be found to have held, with one mind and with one consent, this ought to be accounted the true and Catholic doctrine of the Church, without any doubt or scruple.

[78.] Which lest we should seem to allege presumptuously on our own warrant rather than on the authority of the Church, we appealed to the example of the holy council which some three years ago was held at Ephesus [517] in Asia, in the consulship of Bassus and Antiochus, where, when question was raised as to the authoritative determining of rules of faith, lest, perchance, any profane novelty should creep in, as did the perversion of the truth at Ariminum, [518] the whole body of priests there assembled, nearly two hundred in number, approved of this as the most Catholic, the most trustworthy, and the best course, viz., to bring forth into the midst the sentiments of the holy Fathers, some of whom it was well known had been martyrs, some Confessors, but all had been, and continued to the end to be, Catholic priests, in order that by their consentient determination the reverence due to ancient truth might be duly and solemnly confirmed, and the blasphemy of profane novelty condemned. Which having been done, that impious Nestorius was lawfully and deservedly adjudged to be opposed to Catholic antiquity, and contrariwise blessed Cyril to be in agreement with it. And that nothing might be wanting to the credibility of the matter, we recorded the names and the number (though we had forgotten the order) of the Fathers, according to whose consentient and unanimous judgment, both the sacred preliminaries of judicial procedure were expounded, and the rule of divine truth established. Whom, that we may strengthen our memory, it will be no superfluous labour to mention again here also.

[517] The Council of Ephesus, summoned by the Emperor Theodosius to meet at Whitsuntide, 431 (June 7), held its first sitting on June 22, in the Church of St. Mary, where the blessed Virgin was believed to have been buried.

[518] See note above, p. 131, n. 3.

Chapter XXX.
The Council of Ephesus.

[79.] These then are the men whose writings, whether as judges or as witnesses, were recited in the Council: St. Peter, bishop of Alexandria, a most excellent Doctor and most blessed martyr, Saint Athanasius, bishop of the same city, a most faithful Teacher, and most eminent Confessor, Saint Theophilus, also bishop of the same city, a man illustrious for his faith, his life, his knowledge, whose successor, the revered Cyril, now [519] adorns the Alexandrian Church. And lest perchance the doctrine ratified by the Council should be thought peculiar to one city and province, there were added also those lights of Cappadocia, St. Gregory of Nazianzus, bishop and Confessor, St. Basil of Caesarea in Cappadocia, bishop and Confessor, and the other St. Gregory, St. Gregory of Nyssa, for his faith, his conversation, his integrity, and his wisdom, most worthy to be the brother of Basil. And lest Greece or the East should seem to stand alone, to prove that the Western and Latin world also have always held the same belief, there were read in the Council certain Epistles of St. Felix, martyr, and St. Julius, both bishops of Rome. And that not only the Head, but the other parts, of the world also might bear witness to the judgment of the council, there was added from the South the most blessed Cyprian, bishop of Carthage and martyr, and from the North St. Ambrose, bishop of Milan.

[80.] These all then, to the sacred number of the decalogue, [520] were produced at Ephesus as doctors, councillors, witnesses, judges. And that blessed council holding their doctrine, following their counsel, believing their witness, submitting to their judgment without haste, without foregone conclusion, without partiality, gave their determination concerning the Rules of Faith. A much greater number of the ancients might have been adduced; but it was needless, because neither was it fit that the time should be occupied by a multitude of witnesses, nor does any one suppose that those ten were really of a different mind from the rest of their colleagues.

[519] This marks Vincentius's date within very narrow limits, viz. after the Council of Ephesus, and before Cyril's death. Cyril died in 444.

[520] Vincentius's copy of the acts of the Council appears to have contained extracts from no more than ten Fathers. But the Fathers from whose writings extracts were read were twelve in number; the two omitted by Vincentius being Atticus, bishop of Constantinople, and Amphilochius, bishop of Iconium. In Labbe's Concilia, where the whole are given, it is remarked that in one manuscript the two last mentioned occupy a different place from the others. Dean Milman (Latin Christianity, vol. 1, p. 164) speaks of the passages read, "as of very doubtful bearing on the question raised by Nestorius." It is true only two, those from Athanasius and Gregory Nazianzen, contain the crucial term

"Theotocos" but all express the truth which "Theotocos" symbolises. That the word was not of recent introduction, Bishop Pearson (Creed, Art. 3) shows by quotations from other writers besides those produced at the Council, going back as far as to Origen. The Fathers cited may certainly be said to fulfil to some extent Vincentius's requirement of universality. They represent the teaching of Alexandria, Rome, Carthage, Milan, Constantinople, and Asia Minor; but his appeal would have been more to his purpose if antiquity had been more expressly represented. With the exception of Cyprian, all the passages cited were from writers of comparatively recent date at the time, though, as Vincentius truly remarks, others might have been produced. Petavius (De Incarn. l. xiv. c. 15), in defending the cultus of the blessed Virgin and of the saints generally, lays much stress on this omission of citations from earlier Fathers at the Council, as he does also on similar omissions in the case of the fourth, fifth, and sixth Councils, with what object is sufficiently obvious. Bishop Bull points out Petavius's disposition to disparage or misrepresent the teaching of the earlier Fathers, in another and still more important instance. (Defens. Fid. Nic.) Introd. S: 8.

Chapter XXXI.
The Constancy of the Ephesine Fathers in driving away Novelty and maintaining Antiquity.

[81.] After the preceding we added also the sentence of blessed Cyril, which is contained in these same Ecclesiastical Proceedings. For when the Epistle of Capreolus, [521] bishop of Carthage, had been read, wherein he earnestly intreats that novelty may be driven away and antiquity maintained, Cyril made and carried the proposal, which it may not be out of place to insert here: For says he, at the close of the proceedings, "Let the Epistle of Capreolus also, the reverend and very religious bishop of Carthage, which has been read, be inserted in the acts. His mind is obvious, for he intreats that the doctrines of the ancient faith be confirmed, such as are novel, wantonly devised, and impiously promulgated, reprobated and condemned." All the bishops cried out, "These are the words of all; this we all say, this we all desire." What mean "the words of all," what mean "the desires of all," but that what has been handed down from antiquity should be retained, what has been newly devised, rejected with disdain?

[82.] Next we expressed our admiration of the humility and sanctity of that Council, such that, though the number of priests was so great, almost the more part of them metropolitans, so erudite, so learned, that almost all were capable of taking part in doctrinal discussions, whom the very circumstance of their being assembled for the purpose, might seem to embolden to make some determination on their own authority, yet they innovated nothing, presumed nothing, arrogated to themselves absolutely nothing, but used all possible care to hand down nothing to posterity but what they had themselves received from their Fathers. And not only did they dispose satisfactorily of the matter presently in hand, but they also set an example to those who should come after them, how they also should adhere to the determinations of sacred antiquity, and condemn the devices of profane novelty.

[83.] We inveighed also against the wicked presumption of Nestorius in boasting that he was the first and the only one who understood holy Scripture, and that all those teachers were ignorant, who before him had expounded the sacred oracles, forsooth, the whole body of priests, the whole body of Confessors and martyrs, of whom some had published commentaries upon the Law of God, others had agreed with them in their comments, or had acquiesced in them. In a word, he confidently asserted that the whole Church was even now in error, and always had been in error, in that, as it seemed to him, it had followed, and was following, ignorant and misguided teachers.

[521] The letter of Capreolus is given in Labbe's Concilia, vol. 3, col. 529 sqq. The Emperor Theodosius had written to Augustine, requiring his presence at the Council which he had summoned to meet at Ephesus in

the matter of Nestorius. But Augustine having died
while the letter was on its way, it was brought to
Capreolus, bishop of Carthage and Metropolitan.
Capreolus would have summoned a meeting of the
African bishops, that they might appoint a delegate to
represent them at the Council; but the presence of the
hostile Vandals, who were laying waste the country in all
directions, made it impossible for the bishops to travel
to any place of meeting. Capreolus therefore could do
no more than send his deacon Besula to represent him
and the African Church, bearing with him the letter
referred to in the text. The letter, after having been read
before the Council, both in the original Latin and in a
Greek translation, was, on the motion of Cyril, inserted
in the acts.

Chapter XXXII.
The zeal of Celestine and Sixtus, bishops of Rome, in opposing Novelty.

[84.] The foregoing would be enough and very much more than enough, to crush and annihilate every profane novelty. But yet that nothing might be wanting to such completeness of proof, we added, at the close, the twofold authority of the Apostolic See, first, that of holy Pope Sixtus, the venerable prelate who now adorns the Roman Church; and secondly that of his predecessor, Pope Celestine of blessed memory, which same we think it necessary to insert here also.

Holy Pope Sixtus [522] then says in an Epistle which he wrote on Nestorius's matter to the bishop of Antioch, "Therefore, because, as the Apostle says, the faith is one,--evidently the faith which has obtained hitherto,-- let us believe the things that are to be said, and say the things that are to be held." What are the things that are to be believed and to be said? He goes on: "Let no license be allowed to novelty, because it is not fit that any addition should be made to antiquity. Let not the clear faith and belief of our forefathers be fouled by any muddy admixture." A truly apostolic sentiment! He enhances the belief of the Fathers by the epithet of clearness; profane novelties he calls muddy.

[85.] Holy Pope Celestine also expresses himself in like manner and to the same effect. For in the Epistle which he wrote to the priests of Gaul, charging them with connivance with error, in that by their silence they failed in their duty to the ancient faith, and allowed profane novelties to spring up, he says: "We are deservedly to blame if we encourage error by silence. Therefore rebuke these people. Restrain their liberty of preaching." But here some one may doubt who they are whose liberty to preach as they list he forbids,--the preachers of antiquity or the devisers of novelty. Let himself tell us; let himself resolve the reader's doubt. For he goes on: "If the case be so (that is, if the case be so as certain persons complain to me touching your cities and provinces, that by your hurtful dissimulation you cause them to consent to certain novelties), if the case be so, let novelty cease to assail antiquity." This, then, was the sentence of blessed Celestine, not that antiquity should cease to subvert novelty, but that novelty should cease to assail antiquity. [523]

[522] Sixtus III. See the Epistle in Labbe's Concilia, T. iii. Col. 1262.

[523] Celestine's letter will be found in the appendix to Vol. x., Part II., of St. Augustine's Works, col. 2403, Paris 1838. See the remarks on Vincentius's mode of dealing with Celestine's letter, Appendix III.

Chapter XXXIII.
The Children of the Catholic Church ought to adhere to the Faith of their Fathers and die for it.

[86.] Whoever then gainsays these Apostolic and Catholic determinations, first of all necessarily insults the memory of holy Celestine, who decreed that novelty should cease to assail antiquity; and in the next place sets at naught the decision of holy Sixtus, whose sentence was, "Let no license be allowed to novelty, since it is not fit that any addition be made to antiquity;" moreover, he condemns the determination of blessed Cyril, who extolled with high praise the zeal of the venerable Capreolus, in that he would fain have the ancient doctrines of the faith confirmed, and novel inventions condemned; yet more, he tramples upon the Council of Ephesus, that is, on the decisions of the holy bishops of almost the whole East, who decreed, under divine guidance, that nothing ought to be believed by posterity save what the sacred antiquity of the holy Fathers, consentient in Christ, had held, who with one voice, and with loud acclaim, testified that these were the words of all, this was the wish of all, this was the sentence of all, that as almost all heretics before Nestorius, despising antiquity and upholding novelty, had been condemned, so Nestorius, the author of novelty and the assailant of antiquity, should be condemned also. Whose consentient determination, inspired by the gift of sacred and celestial grace, whoever disapproves must needs hold the profaneness of Nestorius to have been condemned unjustly; finally, he despises as vile and worthless the whole Church of Christ, and its doctors, apostles, and prophets, and especially the blessed Apostle Paul: he despises the Church, in that she hath never failed in loyalty to the duty of cherishing and preserving the faith once for all delivered to her; he despises St. Paul, who wrote, "O Timothy, guard the deposit intrusted to thee, shunning profane novelties of words;" [524] and again, "if any man preach unto you other than ye have received, let him be accursed." [525] But if neither apostolical injunctions nor ecclesiastical decrees may be violated, by which, in accordance with the sacred consent of universality and antiquity, all heretics always, and, last of all, Pelagius, Coelestius, and Nestorius have been rightly and deservedly condemned, then assuredly it is incumbent on all Catholics who are anxious to approve themselves genuine sons of Mother Church, to adhere henceforward to the holy faith of the holy Fathers, to be wedded to it, to die in it; but as to the profane novelties of profane men--to detest them, abhor them, oppose them, give them no quarter.

[87.] These matters, handled more at large in the two preceding Commonitories, I have now put together more briefly by way of recapitulation, in order that my memory, to aid which I composed them, may, on the one hand, be refreshed by frequent reference, and, on the other, may avoid being wearied by prolixity.

[524] 1 Tim. vi. 20.

[525] Gal. i. 9.

Appendix I.

Note on Section 41, Page 143.

There is so close an agreement, both in substance and often in the form of expression, between the preceding sections (36-42) and the so-called Athanasian Creed, that it led Antelmi (Nova de Symb. Athanas. Disquisitio,) to ascribe that document to Vincentius as its author, and to suppose that in it we have the fulfilment of the promise here referred to. If, however, the Creed was the work of Vincentius, it cannot well be the work promised at the close of S: 41, for Vincentius's words point to a fuller and more explicit treatment of the subjects referred to, whereas in the Athanasian Creed, though the subjects are the same, the treatment of them is very much briefer and more concise.

Whoever was the author however, if it was not Vincentius, he must at least, as the subjoined extracts seem to prove, have been familiar with the Commonitory, as also with St. Augustine's writings, of which, as well as of the Commonitory, the Creed bears evident traces. I subjoin the following instances of agreement between the Commonitory and the Creed: Antelmi gives several others.

Commonitory:

Athanasian Creed:

Unum Christum Jesum, non duos, eumdemque Deum pariter atque Hominem confitetur. S: 36.

Est ergo Fides recta, ut credamus et confiteamur, quia Dominus noster Jesus Christus, Dei Filius, Deus pariter et Homo est. v. 28.

Alia est Persona Patris, alia Filii, alia Spiritus Sancti. S: 37.

Alia est Persona Patris, alia Filii, alia Spiritus Sancti. v. 5.

Unus idemque Christus, Deus et Homo, Idem Patri et aequalis et minor, Idem ex Patre ante saecula genitus, Idem in saeculo ex Matre generatus, perfectus Deus, perfectus Homo. S: 37.

Deus ex substantia Patris, ante saecula genitus, Homo ex substantia Matris, in saeculo natus; perfectus Deus perfectus Homo. vv. 29, 30.

Unus, non corruptibili nescio qua Divinitatis et Humanitatis confusione, sed integra et singulari quadam unitate Personae. S: 37.

Unus omnino, non conversione sustantiae, sed unitate Personae. v. 34.

Sicut Verbum in carne caro, ita Homo in Deo Deus est. S: 40.

Unus, non conversione Divinitatis in carne, sed Adsumptione Humanitatis in Deo. [526] v. 33.

[526] This is probably the true reading.

Appendix II.

Note on Section 69, Page 149.

That Vincentius had Augustine and his adherents in view
in this description will hardly be doubted by any one
who will compare it with the following extracts, the first
from Prosper's letter to Augustine, [527] giving him an
account of the complaints made against his doctrine by
the Massilian clergy; the second from St. Augustine's
treatise, "De dono Perseveranti " [528] written in
consequence of it.

Commonitory, S: 69.

"Si quis interroget quempiam haereticorum sibi talia
persuadentem, Unde probas, unde doces quod Ecclesiae
Catholicae universalem et antiquam fidem dimittere
debeam? Statum ille, Scriptum est enim,' et continuo
mille testimonia, mille exempla, mille auctoritates parat
de Lege, de Psalmis, de Apostolis, de Prophetis, quibus,
novo et malo more interpretatis, ex arce Catholica in
haereseos barathrum infelix anima praecipitetur. Audent
enim polliceri et docere, quod in Ecclesia sua, id est, in
communionis suae conventiculo, magna et specialis ac
plane personalis quaedam sit Dei gratia, adeo ut sine ullo
labore, sine ullo studio, sine ulla industria, etiamsi nec
petant, nec quaerant, nec pulsent, quicunque illi ad
numerum suum pertinent, tamen ita divinitus

dispensentur, ut, angelicis evecti manibus, id est, angelica protectione servati, nunquam possint offendere ad lapidem pedem suum, id est, nunquam scandalizari."

Prosper to Augustine.

"The Massilian clergy complain," he says, "Romoveri omnem industriam, tollique virtutes, si Dei constitutio humanus praeveniat voluntates." S: 3.

Then referring to the teaching of the Massilians themselves, Prosper continues,

"Ad conditionem hanc velint uniuscujusque hominis pertinere, ut ad cognitionem Dei et ad obedientiam mandatorum Ejus possit suam dirigere voluntatem, et ad hanc gratiam qua in Christo renascimur pervenire, per naturalem scilicet facultatem, petendo, quaerendo, pulsando."

Referring to the line of argument pursued by himself and others of Augustine's friends and the Massilian way of dealing with it, he says, "Et cum contra eos Scripta Beatitudinis tuae validissimis et innumeris testimoniis Divinarum Scriptuarum instructa proferimus,...obstinationem suam vetustate defendunt." S: 3.

St. Augustine replies to Prosper not in an ordinary letter, but in two short Treatises, which must have been written immediately afters its receipt, for he died in August 430, the first entitled "De Praedestinatione Sanctorum," the second "De Dono Perseverantiae."

The following extract is from the latter:

"Attendant ergo quomodo falluntur qui putant Esse a nobis, non dari nobis, ut petamus, quaeramus, pulsemus. Et hoc esse, dicunt, quod gratia praeceditur merito nostro, ut sequatur illa cum accipimus petentes, et invenimus quaerentes, aperiturque pulsantibus. Nec volunt intelligere etiam hoc divini muneris esse ut oremus, hoc est, petamus, quaeramus, atque pulsamus."--De Dono Persev. c. 23, S: 64.

Vincentius's language is in keeping with that of others of St. Augustine's opponents, as Cassian and Faustus, extracts from whom are given by Noris; only, as he observes, while Vincentius uses the term "heresy" of the doctrine impugned,--they are content to use the milder term "error."--Histor. Pelag. p. 246.

[527] Inter Epistolas S. August. Ep. 225. Tom. ii. and again Tom. x. col. 1327.

[528] Opera ix. col. 1833.

Appendix III.

Note on Section 85, Page 156.

Celestine's letter was addressed to certain Bishops of Southern Gaul, who are particularized by name.

It appears that Prosper and Hilary had made a journey to Rome, where they then were, for the purpose of complaining to Celestine of the connivance of certain bishops of Southern Gaul with the unsound teaching of their clergy. They complained too of the disrespectful manner in which these same clergy treated the memory of Augustine, then recently deceased.

Celestine writes to these bishops: blames their connivance with a fault, which, says he, by their silence they make their own, and then proceeds to charge them, as in the passage quoted in the text, "Rebuke these people: restrain their liberty of preaching. If the case be so, let novelty cease to assail antiquity, let restlessness cease to disturb the Church's peace." Then, after some further exhortation, he adds, "We cannot wonder at their thus assailing the living, when they do not shrink from seeking to asperse the memory of the departed. With Augustine, whom all men everywhere loved and honoured, we ever held communion. Let a stop be put to this spirit of disparagement, which unhappily is on the increase."

The manner in which Vincentius deals with this letter has been very commonly thought, and with reason, to indicate a Semipelagian leaning. [529] His "si ita est," "if the case be so," emphasized by being repeated again and again, quite in an excited manner, as we should say, shows an evident wish to shift the charge of novelty from those against whom it had been brought, and fix it upon the opposite party. "Who are the introducers of novelty? The Massilians, as Prosper represents them, or their calumniators? Not the Massilians: they notoriously appeal to antiquity,--not the Massilians, but Prosper and the rest of Augustine's followers."

The feeling with regard to Augustine, on the part of the Massilian clergy, as indicated in Celestine's letter, is quite in accordance with the animus of S: 69 above. See the note on that place, and see Noris's remarks, pp. 246-248.

[529] E.g. "Hunc locum Vincentius Lirinensis sic a vero sensu contra Prosperum et Hilarium detorquet, ut ipse haud injuria in erroris Semipelagiani suspicionem veniat." The Benedictine editor of St. Augustine's works on Celestine's letter, Tom. x. col. 2403. To the same purpose, among others, Card. Norris, Histor. Pelag., 246. Vossius, Histor. Pelag. Tillemont, T. xv. pp. 145, 862. Neander, Church History, iv. p. 388.